THE UNITED METHODIST
BOOK OF WORSHIP

PASTOR'S
POCKET
EDITION

THE UNITED METHODIST PUBLISHING HOUSE
NASHVILLE, TENNESSEE

THE UNITED METHODIST BOOK OF WORSHIP
Pastor's Pocket Edition

Pastor's Pocket Edition ISBN 978-0-687-03575-5

Pastor's Pocket Edition (ePub) ISBN 978-0-687-01962-5
Hardcover (black) ISBN 978-0-687-03572-4
Genuine Leather (black) ISBN 978-0-687-03573-1
Accompaniment PDF Download ISBN 978-1-501-80068-9

Scripture, unless otherwise indicated, is adapted from the New Revised Standard Version of the Bible, copyright © 1989 by the Division of Christian Education of the National Council of Churches of Christ in the USA and is used by permission.

19 20 21 22 — 29 28 27 26

PRINTED IN CHINA

TERMS, ABBREVIATIONS,
AND SYMBOLS

UMH is the abbreviation for *The United Methodist Hymnal.*

Numbers preceded by *UMH* refer to *The United Methodist Hymnal.*

Scripture references are listed in lectionary order: (1) Old Testament lessons, (2) Psalms, (3) New Testament lessons other than the Gospels, and (4) Gospel lessons.

Brackets [ ] indicate an act of worship that is ordinarily included but may be omitted in some situations.

"Leader" means a worship leader, who may be either lay or clergy.

CONTENTS

A SERVICE OF WORD AND TABLE V
WITH PERSONS WHO ARE SICK
OR HOMEBOUND

Since the earliest Christian times, communion has been brought as an extension of the congregation's worship to sick or homebound persons unable to attend congregational worship.

The following service is very flexible, depending upon the circumstances of the pastoral visit. "The people" may be simply the pastor and one other person. The service may be very informal and conversational. There should be every possible sensitivity to the particular needs of the person(s) receiving communion.

The pastor, or laypersons at the direction of the pastor, may distribute the consecrated bread and cup to sick or homebound persons as soon as feasible following a service of Word and Table as an extension of that service. When this service is used as a distribution of the consecrated bread and cup, the Great Thanksgiving is omitted, but thanks should be given after the bread and cup are received.

There should be whatever participation is feasible by those receiving communion. Sometimes this may simply be gestures and expression. Familiar acts of worship that persons may know by memory—the Lord's Prayer, the Apostles' Creed, or the Twenty-third Psalm, for instance—may be used. Sometimes it is possible to sing one or more hymns.

Those distributing communion should also be sensitive to the power of acts such as calling the person by name, touching the person, encouraging the remembrance of significant experiences, and allowing sick or homebound persons to minister to the visitors.

The people come together and exchange greetings in the Lord's name.

Scriptures are read and interpreted, and prayer and praise are offered.

INVITATION

Christ our Lord invites to his table
    all who love him and seek to grow into his likeness.
Let us draw near with faith, make our humble confession,
    and prepare to receive this Holy Sacrament.

CONFESSION AND PARDON

We do not presume to come to this your table, merciful Lord,

**trusting in our own goodness, but in your unfailing mercies.
We are not worthy that you should receive us,
but give your word and we shall be healed,
through Jesus Christ our Lord. Amen.**

Hear the good news:
   Christ died for us while we were yet sinners;
   that is proof of God's love toward us.
In the name of Jesus Christ, you are forgiven!

THE PEACE

Signs and words of God's peace are exchanged.

TAKING THE BREAD AND CUP

The bread and wine are prepared for the meal.

THE GREAT THANKSGIVING

*The pastor prays as follows if the bread and cup are to be consecrated.
If they have already been consecrated, this prayer is omitted.*

*If a layperson is distributing the consecrated bread and cup, this
prayer is omitted.*

Lift up your heart(s) and give thanks to the Lord our God.

Father Almighty, Creator of heaven and earth,
   you made us in your image, to love and be loved.
When we turned away, and our love failed,
   your love remained steadfast.
By the suffering, death, and resurrection
   of your only Son Jesus Christ
   you delivered us from slavery to sin and death
   and made with us a new covenant by water and the Spirit.

On the night in which Jesus gave himself up for us he took bread,
   gave thanks to you, broke the bread, gave it to his disciples,
   and said: "Take, eat; this is my body which is given for you.
   Do this in remembrance of me."

When the supper was over he took the cup,
   gave thanks to you, gave it to his disciples, and said:
"Drink from this, all of you; this is my blood of the new covenant,
   poured out for you and for many for the forgiveness of sins.
Do this, as often as you drink it, in remembrance of me."

And so, in remembrance of these your mighty acts in Jesus
Christ, we offer ourselves in praise and thanksgiving

as a holy and living sacrifice,
    in union with Christ's offering for us.
Pour out your Holy Spirit on us,
    and on these gifts of bread and wine.
Make them be for us the body and blood of Christ,
    that we may be for the world the body of Christ,
    redeemed by his blood.

By your Spirit make us one with Christ, one with each other,
    and one in ministry to all the world,
until Christ comes in final victory,
    and we feast at his heavenly banquet.
Through your Son Jesus Christ,
    with the Holy Spirit in your holy Church,
all honor and glory is yours, almighty Father, now and for ever.
    Amen.

THE LORD'S PRAYER

BREAKING THE BREAD

In silence or with appropriate words.

GIVING THE BREAD AND CUP

With these or other words being exchanged:

Name, the body of Christ, given for you. **Amen.**
Name, the blood of Christ, given for you. **Amen.**

When all have received, the Lord's table is put in order.

*Thanks may be given after communion. A hymn or chorus may be
sung. If the consecrated bread and cup have been given and there has
been no Great Thanksgiving, the following prayer is suggested after
Communion:*

Most bountiful God,
    we give you thanks for the world you have created,
    for the gift of life, and for giving yourself to us in Jesus Christ,
    whose holy life, suffering and death, and glorious resurrection
    have delivered us from slavery to sin and death.
We thank you that in the power of your Holy Spirit
    you have fed us in this Sacrament, united us with Christ,
    and given us a foretaste of your heavenly banquet.
We are your children, and yours is the glory, now and for ever;
through Jesus Christ our Lord. **Amen.**

BLESSING

The grace of the Lord Jesus Christ,
and the love of God,
and the communion of the Holy Spirit
be with you [all]. **Amen.**

SERVICES OF THE
BAPTISMAL COVENANT

THE BAPTISMAL COVENANT II-A

A BRIEF ORDER OF HOLY BAPTISM
FOR CHILDREN AND OTHERS UNABLE
TO ANSWER FOR THEMSELVES

*This service is designed for situations when the persons baptized are
(1) children who cannot take their own vows or (2) youths or adults
who have not reached the developmental stage of making decisions for
themselves. It is not designed for the baptism of persons who take their
own vows, or for confirmation or reaffirmation of faith.*

INTRODUCTION OF THE SERVICE
  AND PRESENTATION OF CANDIDATE(S)

RENUNCIATION OF SIN AND PROFESSION OF FAITH

The pastor addresses parents or other sponsors:

On behalf of the whole Church, I ask you:
Do you reject all that is evil, repent of your sin,
and accept the freedom and power God gives you
  to resist evil, injustice, and oppression
  in whatever forms they present themselves?

I do.

Do you confess Jesus Christ as your Savior,
put your whole trust in his grace,
and promise to serve him as your Lord,
in union with the Church which Christ has opened
  to people of all ages, nations, and races?

I do.

Will you nurture *these children (persons)* in Christ's holy Church,
that by your teaching and example *they* may be guided
  to accept God's grace for *themselves*,
  to profess *their* faith openly,
  and to lead a Christian life?

I will.

11

The pastor addresses the congregation, and the congregation responds:

Do you, as Christ's body, the Church,
reaffirm both your rejection of sin and your commitment to Christ?

We do.

Will you nurture one another in the Christian faith and life,
include *these persons* now before you in your care,
and surround *them* with a community of love and forgiveness?

We will.

THANKSGIVING OVER THE WATER

Eternal Father, your mighty acts of salvation
   have been made known through water—
from the moving of your Spirit upon the waters of creation,
to the deliverance of your people
   through the flood and through the Red Sea.
In the fullness of time you sent Jesus,
   nurtured in the water of a womb,
   baptized by John, and anointed by your Spirit.
He called his disciples
   to share in the baptism of his death and resurrection
    and to make disciples of all nations.
Pour out your Holy Spirit,
   to bless this gift of water and *those* who *receive* it,
   to wash away *their* sin and clothe *them* in righteousness
    throughout *their lives*
that, dying and being raised with Christ,
   they may share in his final victory;
through the same Jesus Christ our Lord. **Amen.**

BAPTISM WITH LAYING ON OF HANDS

As each candidate is baptized, the pastor uses the Christian name(s), but not the surname:

Christian Name(s), I baptize you in the name of the Father,
   and of the Son,
   and of the Holy Spirit. **Amen.**

Immediately after the administration of the water, the pastor places hands on the candidate's head and invokes the work of the Holy Spirit. Other persons, including baptized members of the candidate's family, may join the pastor in this action. During the laying on of hands, the pastor says:

The Holy Spirit work within you,
that being born through water and the Spirit,
you may be a faithful disciple of Jesus Christ. Amen.

COMMENDATION AND WELCOME

The pastor may invite the congregation to participate by turning to item 16 on UMH 38.

Those who have been baptized into Christ's holy Church are now welcomed into this congregation of The United Methodist Church.

The pastor addresses the congregation:

Members of the household of God,
I commend these persons to your love and care.
Do all in your power to increase their faith,
confirm their hope, and perfect them in love.

The congregation responds:

We give thanks for all that God has already given you
 and we welcome you in Christian love.
As members together with you
 in the body of Christ
 and in this congregation
 of The United Methodist Church,
we renew our covenant
 faithfully to participate
 in the ministries of the Church
 by our prayers, our presence,
 our gifts, our service, and our witness
 that in everything God may be glorified
 through Jesus Christ.

The pastor addresses those baptized and their parents and sponsors:

The God of all grace,
 who has called us to eternal glory in Christ,
establish you and strengthen you
 by the power of the Holy Spirit,
that you may live in grace and peace.

One or more laypersons, including children, may join the pastor in acts of welcome and peace. Baptized children may be welcomed by a kiss of peace or other acts or words immediately following Baptism with Laying on of Hands. Then an appropriate hymn, stanza, or response may be sung.

Appropriate thanksgivings and intercessions for those who have participated in these acts should be included in the Concerns and Prayers that follow. It is most fitting that the service continue with Holy Communion, in which the union of the newly baptized children with the body of Christ is most fully expressed.

THE BAPTISMAL COVENANT II-B

HOLY BAPTISM
FOR CHILDREN AND OTHERS UNABLE
TO ANSWER FOR THEMSELVES

This text from the rituals of the former Methodist and former Evangelical United Brethren churches is used by the pastor while the congregation uses The Congregational Pledge 1 or 2 (UMH 44).

It is designed for use when the only persons being baptized are (1) children who cannot take their own vows or (2) youths or adults who have not reached the developmental stage of making decisions for themselves. It is not designed for the baptism of persons who take their own vows, or for confirmation or reaffirmation of faith.

INTRODUCTION TO THE SERVICE

As persons come forward, an appropriate baptismal hymn may be sung.

The pastor addresses the congregation:

Dearly beloved,
baptism is an outward and visible sign
  of the grace of the Lord Jesus Christ,
through which grace
  we became partakers of his righteousness
  and heirs of life eternal.
Those receiving the Sacrament
  are thereby marked as Christian disciples,
  and initiated into the fellowship of Christ's holy Church.
Our Lord has expressly given to little children
  a place among the people of God,
  which holy privilege must not be denied them.
Remember the words of the Lord Jesus Christ, how he said,
  "Let the children come to me, do not hinder them;
  for to such belongs the kingdom of God."

PROFESSION OF FAITH

The pastor addresses parents or other sponsors:

Beloved,
do you in presenting *these children (persons)* for Holy Baptism
    confess your faith in our Lord and Savior Jesus Christ?

I do.

Do you therefore accept as your bounden duty and privilege
to live before *these children (persons)*
    a life that becomes the Gospel;
to exercise all godly care
    that *they* be brought up in the Christian faith,
    that *they* be taught the Holy Scriptures,
    and that *they* learn to give reverent attendance
        upon the private and public worship of God?

I do.

Will you endeavor to keep *these children (persons)*
    under the ministry and guidance of the Church
until *they* by the power of God
    shall accept for *themselves* the gift of salvation,
    and be confirmed
    as *full and responsible members* of Christ's holy Church?

I will.

BAPTISM

The pastor asks the parent(s) or sponsor(s) of each candidate:

What name is given this *child (person)?*

*Then, repeating the name(s), though not including the surname, the
pastor baptizes each candidate, saying:*

Christian Name(s), I baptize you in the name of the Father,
    and of the Son,
    and of the Holy Spirit. **Amen.**

CONGREGATIONAL PLEDGE

*The pastor addresses the congregation, and the congregation re-
sponds with The Congregational Pledge 1 or 2 (UMH 44), as
follows:*

The Congregational Pledge 1

Do you as a congregation accept the responsibility
    of assisting *these parents (and sponsors)*

in fulfillment of the baptismal vows,
and do you undertake to provide facilities and opportunities
for Christian nurture and fellowship?

We will, by the grace of God.

The Congregational Pledge 2

Members of the household of faith,
I commend to your love and care *these children (persons)*,
  whom we this day recognize as *members* of the family of
    God.
Will you endeavor so to live
that *these children (persons)* may grow
  in the knowledge and love of God,
through our Savior Jesus Christ?

With God's help
we will so order our lives after the example of Christ,
that *these children (persons)*, surrounded by steadfast love,
may be established in the faith,
and confirmed and strengthened
in the way that leads to life eternal.

PRAYER

Let us pray.

O God, our heavenly Father,
grant that *these children (persons)*, as *they grow* in years,
  may also grow in grace
  and in the knowledge of the Lord Jesus Christ,
and that
  by the restraining and renewing influence of the Holy Spirit
    they may ever be *true children* of thine,
  serving these faithfully all *their* days.
So guide and uphold
  the *parents/sponsors* of *these children (persons)*
that, by loving care, wise counsel, and holy example,
  they may lead *them* into that life of faith
    whose strength is righteousness
  and whose fruit is everlasting joy and peace;
through Jesus Christ our Lord. **Amen.**

BLESSING

God the Father, God the Son, and God the Holy Spirit bless,
preserve, and keep you, now and for evermore. **Amen.**

One or more laypersons, including children, may join the pastor in acts of welcome and peace. Baptized children may be welcomed by a kiss of peace or other acts or words immediately following Baptism.

Then an appropriate hymn, stanza, or response may be sung.

Appropriate thanksgivings and intercessions for those who have participated in these acts should be included in the Concerns and Prayers that follow.

It is most fitting that the service continue with Holy Communion, in which the union of the newly baptized children with the body of Christ is most fully expressed.

SERVICES OF
CHRISTIAN MARRIAGE

A SERVICE OF CHRISTIAN MARRIAGE I

This service of Christian marriage is found in UMH 864-69. It is provided for couples who wish to solemnize their marriage in a service of Christian worship, parallel in its structure to the Sunday service, which includes the proclamation of the Word with prayer and praise. Christian marriage is proclaimed as a sacred covenant reflecting the Baptismal Covenant. Everything about the service is designed to witness that this is a Christian marriage.

Both words and actions consistently reflect the belief that husband and wife are equal partners in Christian marriage and that they are entering into the marriage of their own volition.

Those present are understood to be an active congregation rather than simply passive witnesses. They give their blessing to the couple and to the marriage, and they join in prayer and praise. It is highly appropriate that the congregation sing hymns and other acts of worship. See the wedding hymns in UMH 642-47 and those listed under Weddings in UMH 953-54.

Holy Communion may or may not be celebrated. If it is, it is most important that its significance be made clear. Specifically: (1) The marriage rite is included in a Service of Word and Table. (2) Not only the husband and wife but the whole congregation are to be invited to receive communion. It is our tradition to invite all Christians to the Lord's table. (3) There should be no pressure that would embarrass those who for whatever reason do not choose to receive communion.

The decision to perform the ceremony is the right and responsibility of the pastor, in accordance with the laws of the state and The United Methodist Church. All plans should be approved by the pastor. The pastor's "due counsel with the parties involved" prior to marriage, mandated by The Book of Discipline, should include, in addition to premarital counseling, discussing and planning the service with them and informing them of policies or guidelines established by the congregation on such matters as decorations, photography, and audio or video recording. Any leadership roles taken by other clergy should be at the invitation of the pastor of the church where the service is held. The organist or person in charge of the music should be consulted and work with the couple in all decisions on music selection.

18

Ethnic and cultural traditions are encouraged and may be incorporated into the service at the discretion of the pastor.

Any children of the man or the woman, other family, and friends may take a variety of roles in the service, depending on their ages and abilities. They may, for example, be members of the wedding party, participate in the Response of the Families and People, read scripture lessons, sing or play instrumental music, or make a witness in their own words.

In the case of couples who are not church members or are not prepared to make the Christian commitment expressed in our services, adaptations may be made at the discretion of the pastor.

ENTRANCE

The congregation may participate by using A Service of Christian Marriage in UMH 864.

GATHERING

While the people gather, instrumental or vocal music may be offered.

Here and throughout the service, the use of music appropriate for Christian worship is strongly encouraged.

During the entrance of the wedding party, there may be instrumental music or a hymn, a psalm, a canticle, or an anthem. The congregation may be invited to stand.

The woman and the man, entering separately or together, now come forward with members of the wedding party. The woman and the man may be escorted by representatives of their families until they have reached the front of the church, or through the Response of the Families, at which time their escorts are seated.

GREETING

Pastor to people:

Friends, we are gathered together in the sight of God
to witness and bless the joining together of
   Name and *Name* in Christian marriage.
The covenant of marriage was established by God,
   who created us male and female for each other.
With his presence and power
   Jesus graced a wedding at Cana of Galilee,
and in his sacrificial love
   gave us the example for the love of husband and wife.

Name and *Name* come to give themselves to one another
   in this holy covenant.

DECLARATION OF INTENTION

DECLARATION BY THE MAN AND THE WOMAN

Pastor to the persons who are to marry:

I ask you now, in the presence of God and these people,
to declare your intention
to enter into union with each other
through the grace of Jesus Christ,
   who calls you into union with himself
   as acknowledged in your baptism.

Pastor to the woman:

Name, will you have *Name* to be your husband,
   to live together in holy marriage?
Will you love him, comfort him, honor and keep him,
   in sickness and in health,
and forsaking all others, be faithful to him
   as long as you both shall live?

Woman: **I will.**

Pastor to the man:

Name, will you have *Name* to be your wife,
   to live together in holy marriage?
Will you love her, comfort her, honor and keep her,
   in sickness and in health,
and forsaking all others, be faithful to her
   as long as you both shall live?

Man: **I will.**

RESPONSE OF THE FAMILIES AND PEOPLE

Pastor to people:

The marriage of *Name* and *Name* unites their families
   and creates a new one.
They ask for your blessing.

*Parents and other representatives of the families may respond in one
of the following ways:*

**We rejoice in your union,
and pray God's blessing upon you.**

or, in reply to the pastor's question:

Do you who represent their families
rejoice in their union
and pray God's blessing upon them?

We do.

*or, children of the couple may repeat these or similar words, prompted
line by line, by the pastor:*

We love both of you.
We bless your marriage.
Together we will be a family.

*If the woman and the man have been escorted by representatives of
their families, their escorts, having blessed the marriage in the name
of their families, may be seated.*

Pastor to people:

Will all of you, by God's grace,
do everything in your power
to uphold and care for these two persons in their marriage?

People: **We will.**

PRAYER

The Lord be with you.
And also with you.
Let us pray.

God of all peoples,
you are the true light illumining everyone.
You show us the way, the truth, and the life.
You love us even when we are disobedient.
You sustain us with your Holy Spirit.
We rejoice in your life in the midst of our lives.
We praise you for your presence with us,
  and especially in this act of solemn covenant;
through Jesus Christ our Lord. **Amen.**

PROCLAMATION AND RESPONSE

*A hymn, psalm, canticle, anthem, or other music may be offered before
or after the readings. The congregation may be invited to stand.*

Suggested Scripture Lessons

Genesis 1:26-28, 31*a*   The creation of man and woman

Song of Solomon 2:10-14, 16*a*; 8:6-7	Love is as strong as death.
Isaiah 43:1-7	You are precious in God's eyes.
Isaiah 55:10-13	You shall go out in joy.
Isaiah 61:10–62:3	Rejoice in the Lord.
Isaiah 63:7-9	The steadfast love of the Lord
Romans 12:1-2, 9-18	The life of a Christian
1 Corinthians 13	The greatest of these is love.
2 Corinthians 5:14-17	In Christ we are a new creation.
Ephesians 2:4-10	God's love for us
Ephesians 4:1-6	Called to the one hope
Ephesians 4:25–5:2	Members one of another
Philippians 2:1-2	The Christlike spirit
Philippians 4:4-9	Rejoice in the Lord.
Colossians 3:12-17	Live in love and thanksgiving.
1 John 3:18-24	Love one another.
1 John 4:7-16	God is love.
Revelation 19:1, 5-9*a*	The wedding feast of the Lamb
Matthew 5:1-10	The Beatitudes
Matthew 7:21, 24-27	A house built upon a rock
Matthew 22:35-40	Love, the greatest commandment
Mark 2:18-22	Joy in Christ as at a wedding
Mark 10:42-45	True greatness
John 2:1-11	The marriage feast of Cana
John 15:9-17	Remain in Christ's love.

SERMON OR OTHER WITNESS TO CHRISTIAN MARRIAGE

INTERCESSORY PRAYER

An extemporaneous prayer may be offered, or the following may be prayed by the pastor or by all:

Eternal God, Creator and Preserver of all life,
  Author of salvation, Giver of all grace:
Bless and sanctify with your Holy Spirit
  Name and *Name*, who come now to join in marriage.
Grant that they may give their vows to each other
  in the strength of your steadfast love.
Enable them to grow in love and peace
  with you and with one another all their days,
  that they may reach out
  in concern and service to the world;
  through Jesus Christ our Lord. **Amen.**

THE MARRIAGE

EXCHANGE OF VOWS

The woman and man face each other, joining hands. The pastor may prompt them, line by line.

Man to woman:

In the name of God,
I, *Name*, take you, *Name*, to be my wife,
   to have and to hold
   from this day forward,
   for better, for worse,
   for richer, for poorer,
   in sickness and in health,
   to love and to cherish,
   until we are parted by death.
This is my solemn vow.

Woman to man:

In the name of God,
I, *Name*, take you, *Name*, to be my husband,
   to have and to hold
   from this day forward,
   for better, for worse,
   for richer, for poorer,
   in sickness and in health,
   to love and to cherish,
   until we are parted by death.
This is my solemn vow.

In place of the vows given above, one of the following may be used:

I take you, *Name*, to be my wife *(husband)*,
   and I promise before God and all who are present here
     to be your loving and faithful husband *(wife)*
     as long as we both shall live.
   I will serve you with tenderness and respect,
   and encourage you to develop God's gifts in you.

Name, in the name of God,
   I take you to be my husband *(wife)* from this time onward,
   to join with you and to share all that is to come,
   to give and to receive,
   to speak and to listen,
   to inspire and to respond,
   and in all our life together

to be loyal to you with my whole being,
as long as we both shall live.

BLESSING AND EXCHANGE OF RINGS

*The exchange of rings is optional. Other tangible symbols may be
given in addition to, or instead of, rings.*

The pastor, taking the rings, may say one of the following:

These rings *(symbols)*
are the outward and visible sign
  of an inward and spiritual grace,
signifying to us the union
  between Jesus Christ and his Church.

These rings *(symbols)*
are the outward and visible sign
  of an inward and spiritual grace,
signifying to all the uniting of *Name* and *Name* in holy marriage.

*The pastor may bless the giving of rings or other symbols of the
  marriage:*

Bless, O Lord, the giving of these rings *(symbols)*,
that they who wear them may live in your peace
  and continue in your favor
  all the days of their life;
through Jesus Christ our Lord. **Amen.**

*While placing the ring on the third finger of the recipient's left hand,
the giver may say (prompted, line by line, by the pastor):*

Name, I give you this *ring*
  as a sign of my vow,
and with all that I am,
  and all that I have,
  I honor you;
in the name of the Father,
  and of the Son,
  and of the Holy Spirit.

*If a unity candle is used, the two side candles representing the
husband and wife are lighted first, and the center candle representing
the marriage is lighted at this or some later point in the service. The
side candles are not extinguished because both husband and wife
retain their personal identities.*

DECLARATION OF MARRIAGE

The wife and husband join hands. The pastor may place a hand on their joined hands.

Pastor to husband and wife:

You have declared your consent and vows
   before God and this congregation.
May God confirm your covenant
   and fill you both with grace.

The couple may turn and face the congregation.

Pastor to people:

Now that *Name* and *Name*
   have given themselves to each other by solemn vows,
   with the joining of hands,
   [and the giving and receiving of *rings*,]

I announce to you that they are husband and wife;
   in the name of the Father,
   and of the Son,
   and of the Holy Spirit.
Those whom God has joined together,
   let no one put asunder. **Amen.**

The congregation may be invited to stand, and a doxology or other hymn may be sung.

Intercessions may be offered for the Church and for the world.

BLESSING OF THE MARRIAGE

The husband and wife may kneel, as the pastor prays:

O God,
you have so consecrated
   the covenant of Christian marriage
   that in it is represented
   the covenant between Christ and his Church.
Send therefore your blessing upon *Name* and *Name*,
   that they may surely keep their marriage covenant,
   and so grow in love and godliness together
   that their home may be a haven of blessing and peace;
through Jesus Christ our Lord. **Amen.**

If Holy Communion is to be celebrated, the congregation turns to A Service of Word and Table III in UMH 15, or one of the musical settings (UMH 17-25), and the service continues with the Thanksgiving and

Communion, below. If Holy Communion is not to be celebrated, the service continues with the following Prayer of Thanksgiving:

Most gracious God,
we give you thanks for your tender love
  in making us a covenant people
  through our Savior Jesus Christ
and for consecrating in his name
  the marriage covenant of *Name* and *Name*.
Grant that their love for each other
  may reflect the love of Christ for us
  and grow from strength to strength
  as they faithfully serve you in the world.
Defend them from every enemy.
Lead them into all peace.
Let their love for each other
  be a seal upon their hearts,
  a mantle about their shoulders,
  and a crown upon their heads.
Bless them
  in their work and in their companionship;
  in their sleeping and in their waking;
  in their joys and in their sorrows;
  in their lives and in their deaths.
Finally, by your grace,
  bring them and all of us to that table
  where your saints feast for ever
  in your heavenly home;
through Jesus Christ our Lord,
  who with you and the Holy Spirit
  lives and reigns,
  one God, for ever and ever. **Amen.**

The Lord's Prayer, prayed by all, using one of the forms in UMH *270-71, 894-96. The wife and husband may continue to kneel.*

The Dismissal with Blessing. See 30.

THANKSGIVING AND COMMUNION

TAKING THE BREAD AND CUP

Pastor to people:

Let us offer ourselves and our gifts to God.

Here the husband and wife, or children from previous marriages, or representatives of the congregation may bring bread and wine to the Lord's table.

The pastor, standing if possible behind the Lord's table, facing the people from this time through Breaking the Bread, takes the bread and cup; and the bread and wine are prepared for the meal.

THE GREAT THANKSGIVING

The Lord be with you.
And also with you.
Lift up your hearts. *The pastor may lift hands and keep them raised.*
We lift them up to the Lord.
Let us give thanks to the Lord our God.
It is right to give our thanks and praise.

It is right, and a good and joyful thing,
   always and everywhere to give thanks to you,
      Father Almighty *(almighty God)*, Creator of heaven and earth.
You formed us in your image, male and female you created us.
You gave us the gift of marriage, that we might fulfill each
   other.

And so,
   with your people on earth and all the company of heaven
   we praise your name and join their unending hymn:

The pastor may lower hands.

Holy, holy, holy Lord, God of power and might,
heaven and earth are full of your glory.
   Hosanna in the highest.
Blessed is he who comes in the name of the Lord.
   Hosanna in the highest.

The pastor may raise hands.

Holy are you, and blessed is your Son Jesus Christ.
By the baptism of his suffering, death, and resurrection
   you gave birth to your Church,
   delivered us from slavery to sin and death,
   and made with us a new covenant
   by water and the Spirit,
      from which flows the covenant love of husband and wife.

The pastor may hold hands, palms down, over the bread, or touch the bread, or lift the bread.

On the night in which he gave himself up for us,
   he took bread, gave thanks to you, broke the bread,

gave it to his disciples, and said:
"Take, eat; this is my body which is given for you.
Do this in remembrance of me."

The pastor may hold hands, palms down, over the cup, or touch the cup, or lift the cup.

When the supper was over he took the cup,
gave thanks to you, gave it to his disciples, and said:
"Drink from this, all of you;
this is my blood of the new covenant,
poured out for you and for many
for the forgiveness of sins.
Do this, as often as you drink it,
in remembrance of me."

The pastor may raise hands.

And so,
in remembrance of these your mighty acts in Jesus Christ,
we offer ourselves in praise and thanksgiving
as a holy and living sacrifice,
in union with Christ's offering for us,
as we proclaim the mystery of faith:

Christ has died; Christ is risen; Christ will come again.

The pastor may hold hands, palms down, over the bread and cup.

Pour out your Holy Spirit on us gathered here,
and on these gifts of bread and wine.
Make them be for us the body and blood of Christ,
that we may be for the world the body of Christ,
redeemed by his blood.

The pastor may extend hands over the husband and wife.

By the same Spirit bless *Name* and *Name*,
that their love for each other
may reflect the love of Christ for us
and grow from strength to strength
as they faithfully serve you in the world.
Defend them from every enemy.
Lead them into all peace.
Let their love for each other
be a seal upon their hearts,
a mantle about their shoulders,
and a crown upon their heads.
Bless them

in their work and in their companionship;
in their sleeping and in their waking;
in their joys and in their sorrows;
in their lives and in their deaths.
Finally, by your grace,
bring them and all of us to that table
  where your saints feast for ever in your heavenly home.

The pastor may raise hands.

Through your Son Jesus Christ,
with the Holy Spirit in your holy Church,
all honor and glory is yours, almighty Father *(God)*,
now and for ever.

Amen.

THE LORD'S PRAYER

The pastor's hands may be extended in open invitation.

And now, with the confidence of children of God, let us pray:

The pastor may raise hands.
All pray the Lord's Prayer, using one of the forms in UMH 270-71,
  894-96.

BREAKING THE BREAD

The pastor, still standing behind the Lord's table facing the people,
breaks the bread and then lifts the cup, in silence or with appropriate
words.

GIVING THE BREAD AND CUP

The bread and wine are given to the people, with these or other words
being exchanged. The husband and wife may assist in the distribution.

The body of Christ, given for you. **Amen.**
The blood of Christ, given for you. **Amen.**

While the bread and wine are given, the congregation may sing
hymns, or there may be vocal or instrumental music. See suggestions
under Weddings or Holy Communion in UMH 953-54, 943.

When all have received, the Lord's table is put in order.

The pastor may then offer the following prayer:

Eternal God, we give you thanks
that you have brought *Name* and *Name*
  [and their families and friends]

together at the table of your family.
Help them grow in love and unity,
that they may rejoice together all the days of their lives
and in the wedding feast of heaven.
Grant this through Jesus Christ our Lord. **Amen.**

SENDING FORTH

Here may be sung a hymn or psalm.

DISMISSAL WITH BLESSING

Pastor to wife and husband:

God the Eternal keep you in love with each other,
so that the peace of Christ may abide in your home.
Go to serve God and your neighbor in all that you do.

Pastor to people:

Bear witness to the love of God in this world,
so that those to whom love is a stranger
will find in you generous friends.
The grace of the Lord Jesus Christ,
and the love of God,
and the communion of the Holy Spirit
be with you all. **Amen.**

THE PEACE

The peace of the Lord be with you always.
And also with you.

The couple may greet each other with a kiss and be greeted by the pastor, after which greetings may be exchanged through the congregation.

GOING FORTH

A hymn may be sung or instrumental music played as the couple, the wedding party, and the people leave.

A SERVICE OF CHRISTIAN MARRIAGE II

This service is a traditional text from the rituals of the former Methodist and former Evangelical United Brethren churches.

The decision to perform the ceremony is the right and responsibility of the pastor, in accordance with the laws of the state and The United

Methodist Church. All plans should be approved by the pastor. The pastor's "due counsel with the parties involved" prior to marriage, mandated by The Book of Discipline, should include, in addition to premarital counseling, discussing and planning the service with them and informing them of policies or guidelines established by the congregation on such matters as decorations, photography, and audio or video recording. Any leadership roles taken by other clergy should be at the invitation of the pastor of the church where the service is held. The organist or person in charge of the music should be consulted and work with the couple in all decisions on music selection. See the wedding hymns in UMH 642-47 and others suggested in A Service of Christian Marriage I.

Ethnic and cultural traditions are encouraged and may be incorporated into the service at the discretion of the pastor.

Any children of the man or the woman, other family, and friends may take a variety of roles in the service, depending on their ages and abilities. They may be members of the wedding party, sing or play instrumental music, or make a witness in their own words. See suggestions for including children in A Service of Christian Marriage I.

In the case of couples who are not church members or are not prepared to make the Christian commitment expressed in our services, adaptations may be made at the discretion of the pastor.

ENTRANCE

GATHERING

While the people gather, instrumental or vocal music may be offered.

Throughout the service, use of specifically Christian music is strongly encouraged.

During the entrance of the wedding party, there may be instrumental music, or a hymn, a psalm, a canticle, or an anthem. The congregation may be invited to stand.

The woman and the man may be escorted by representatives of their families until they have reached the front of the church or until they present the woman and the man, at which time their escorts are seated.

GREETING

Pastor to people:

Dearly beloved,
we are gathered together here in the sight of God,
 and in the presence of these witnesses,
to join together this man and this woman (*Name* and *Name*)

in holy matrimony,
which is an honorable estate, instituted of God,
    and signifying unto us
    the mystical union that exists between Christ and his Church;
which holy estate Christ adorned and beautified
    with his presence in Cana of Galilee.
It is therefore not to be entered into unadvisedly,
    but reverently, discreetly, and in the fear of God.
Into this holy estate these two persons come now to be joined.

DECLARATION OF INTENTION

DECLARATION BY THE MAN AND THE WOMAN

*The pastor gives one of the following charges to the persons who are
to marry:*

I require and charge you both, as you stand in the presence of
    God,
    before whom the secrets of all hearts are disclosed,
    that, having duly considered the holy covenant
        you are about to make,
    you do now declare before this company your pledge of faith,
        each to the other.
Be well assured that if these solemn vows are kept inviolate,
    as God's Word demands,
    and if steadfastly you endeavor
        to do the will of your heavenly Father,
God will bless your marriage,
    will grant you fulfillment in it,
    and will establish your home in peace.

(THE BOOK OF WORSHIP, 1965)

I charge you both, as you stand in the presence of God,
    to remember that love and loyalty alone will avail
    as the foundation of a happy home.
If the solemn vows you are about to make are kept faithfully,
and if steadfastly you endeavor
    to do the will of your heavenly Father,
your life will be full of joy,
    and the home you are establishing will abide in peace.
No other ties are more tender, no other vows more sacred
    than those you now assume.

(EVANGELICAL UNITED BRETHREN, 1959)

Pastor to the man:

Name, will you have this woman to be your wedded wife,
  to live together in the holy estate of matrimony?
Will you love her, comfort her, honor and keep her,
  in sickness and in health;
and forsaking all others keep only to her
  so long as you both shall live?

Man: **I will.**

Pastor to the woman:

Name, will you have this man to be your wedded husband,
  to live together in the holy estate of matrimony?
Will you love him, comfort him, honor and keep him,
  in sickness and in health;
and forsaking all others keep only to him
  so long as you both shall live?

Woman: **I will.**

PRESENTATION

If the woman is presented in marriage, the pastor asks the presenter(s):

Who presents this woman to be married to this man?

Presenter(s): **I (We) do.**

If the man is presented in marriage, the pastor asks the presenter(s):

Who presents this man to be married to this woman?

Presenter(s): **I (We) do.**

The presenter(s) may then be seated.

THE MARRIAGE

EXCHANGE OF VOWS

The woman and man face each other, joining hands. The pastor may prompt them, line by line.

Man to woman:

I, *Name,* take you, *Name,*
  to be my wedded wife,
  to have and to hold,
  from this day forward,
  for better, for worse,
  for richer, for poorer,
  in sickness and in health,

to love and to cherish,
till death us do part,
according to God's holy ordinance;
and thereto I pledge you my faith.

Woman to man:

I, *Name*, take you, *Name*,
to be my wedded husband,
to have and to hold,
from this day forward,
for better, for worse,
for richer, for poorer,
in sickness and in health,
to love and to cherish,
till death us do part,
according to God's holy ordinance;
and thereto I pledge you my faith.

BLESSING AND EXCHANGE OF RINGS

The exchange of rings is optional. Other tangible symbols may be given in addition to, or instead of, rings.

The pastor, taking the rings, may say:

The wedding ring is the outward and visible sign
  of an inward and spiritual grace,
signifying to all
  the uniting of this man and woman in holy matrimony,
  through the Church of Jesus Christ our Lord.

The pastor may bless the giving of rings or other symbols of the marriage:

Bless, O Lord, the giving of these rings,
that they who wear them may abide in thy peace,
  and continue in thy favor;
through Jesus Christ our Lord. **Amen.**

The common custom is for the husband to give the wife her ring before the wife gives the husband his ring. While placing the ring on the third finger of the recipient's left hand, the giver may say (prompted, line by line, by the pastor):

In token and pledge
  of our constant faith and abiding love,
with this ring I thee wed,
in the name of the Father,

and of the Son,
and of the Holy Spirit. **Amen.**

DECLARATION OF MARRIAGE

The wife and husband join hands. The pastor may place a hand on or wrap a stole around their joined hands.

The couple may turn and face the congregation.

Pastor to people:

Forasmuch as *Name* and *Name*
  have consented together in holy wedlock,
  and have witnessed the same before God and this company,
  and thereto have pledged their faith each to the other,
  and have declared the same
    by joining hands and by giving and receiving rings;
I pronounce that they are husband and wife together,
  in the name of the Father,
  and of the Son,
  and of the Holy Spirit.
Those whom God hath joined together, let no one put asunder.
  Amen.

If a unity candle is used, the two side candles representing the husband and wife are lighted first, and the center candle representing the marriage is lighted at this or some later point in the service. The side candles are not extinguished because both husband and wife retain their personal identities.

The congregation may be invited to stand, and a doxology or other hymn may be sung.

BLESSING OF THE MARRIAGE

The husband and wife may kneel, as the pastor prays:

O eternal God,
  creator and preserver of us all,
  giver of all spiritual grace,
  the author of everlasting life:
Send thy blessing upon *Name* and *Name*,
  whom we bless in thy name;
that they may surely perform and keep
  the vow and covenant between them made,
and may ever remain in perfect love and peace together
  and live according to thy laws.
Look graciously upon them,

that they may love, honor, and cherish each other,
and so live together in faithfulness and patience,
   in wisdom and true godliness,
that their home may be a haven of blessing
   and a place of peace;
through Jesus Christ our Lord. **Amen.**

If Holy Communion is not to be celebrated, the service continues as indicated below.

If Holy Communion is to be celebrated, the congregation turns to A Service of Word and Table III in UMH 15 *or one of the musical settings (*UMH 17-25*), and the pastor follows the text on 26-30 above, beginning with Taking the Bread and Cup and concluding with the Dismissal with Blessing on 30 or the one below.*

THE LORD'S PRAYER

The husband and wife may continue to kneel, as all pray the Lord's Prayer.

SENDING FORTH

DISMISSAL WITH BLESSING

God the Father, the Son, and the Holy Spirit
   bless, preserve, and keep you;
the Lord graciously with his favor look upon you,
   and so fill you with all spiritual benediction and love
      that you may so live together in this life
      that in the world to come you may have life everlasting.
   Amen.

The couple may greet each other with a kiss and be greeted by the pastor, after which greetings may be exchanged through the congregation.

GOING FORTH

A hymn may be sung or instrumental music played as the couple, the wedding party, and the people leave.

A SERVICE FOR THE RECOGNITION
OR THE BLESSING OF A
CIVIL MARRIAGE

If this is a separate service of worship at a time other than the regular services of the congregation, the full service below is used.

If this is a Response to the Word in the Sunday service, the usual order may be followed through the sermon. The pastor may then give the Greeting below, or extemporaneous introductory words, followed by the Intercessory Prayer and the remainder of the service.

GATHERING *See 19.*

GREETING

Pastor to people:

Name and *Name* have been married by the law of the state, and
   they have made a solemn contract with each other.
Now, in faith, they come before the witness of the Church to
   declare their marriage covenant
   and to acknowledge God's good news for their lives.

SCRIPTURE LESSON(S)

A hymn, psalm, canticle, anthem, or other music may be offered before or after the readings.

SERMON OR OTHER WITNESS
TO CHRISTIAN MARRIAGE

INTERCESSORY PRAYER

An extemporaneous prayer may be offered, or the following may be prayed by the pastor or by all:

Let us pray.

Eternal God, creator and preserver of all life,
   author of salvation, giver of all grace:
Bless and sanctify with your Holy Spirit *Name* and *Name*,
   who come now asking for your blessing upon their marriage.
Grant that they may reaffirm their vows to each other
   in the strength of your steadfast love.
Enable them to grow in love and peace
   with you and each other all their days,
   that they may reach out

in concern and service to the world;
through Jesus Christ our Lord. **Amen.**

DECLARATION BY THE HUSBAND AND WIFE

Pastor to the husband and wife:

Name and *Name*, you have come here today
  to seek the blessing of God and of the Church
    upon your marriage.

To the wife:

Name, you have taken *Name* to be your lawful husband.
Now you wish to declare, before God and this congregation,
  your desire
    that your married life should be according to God's will.

I ask you, therefore,
will you love him, comfort him, honor and keep him,
  in sickness and in health,
and forsaking all others, be faithful to him
  as long as you both shall live?

Wife: **I will.**

To the husband:

Name, you have taken *Name* to be your lawful wife.
Now you wish to declare, before God and this congregation,
  your desire
    that your married life should be according to God's will.

I ask you, therefore,
will you love her, comfort her, honor and keep her,
  in sickness and in health,
and forsaking all others, be faithful to her
  as long as you both shall live?

Husband: **I will.**

BLESSING OF RINGS

The husband and wife may extend their left hands, and the pastor may place a hand upon the rings and say:

These rings are the outward and visible sign
  of an inward and spiritual grace,
signifying to us the union
  between Jesus Christ and his Church.

The pastor may bless the wearing of rings:

Bless, O Lord, the wearing of these rings
that they who wear them may live in your peace
  and continue in your favor
  all the days of their lives;
through Jesus Christ our Lord. **Amen.**

DECLARATION OF MARRIAGE

The wife and husband join hands. The pastor may place a hand on or wrap a stole around their joined hands. The pastor says to the wife and husband:

Name and *Name*, you are husband and wife
  according to the witness of Christ's universal Church,
  in the name of the Father,
  and of the Son,
  and of the Holy Spirit.
Those whom God has joined together,
  let no one put asunder. **Amen.**

The service continues with the Blessing of the Marriage and all that follows, with or without Holy Communion, in A Service of Christian Marriage I. See 25-30.

AN ORDER FOR THE REAFFIRMATION
OF THE MARRIAGE COVENANT

This order may be a Response to the Word during regular congregational worship, in which case the usual order of Sunday worship may be followed through the sermon. Following the sermon, the pastor invites the couple(s) to come forward, or to stand where they are; and the order below is then followed. Alternatively, a special Service for the Reaffirmation of the Marriage Covenant may be held. It may begin with Gathering and Processional Hymn. Between the Greeting and the Reaffirmation of the Marriage Covenant there may be scripture lessons and praise (see suggestions on 21-22) and a sermon or other witness to Christian marriage. The participating couple(s) should be invited to develop the order and text of the service with the pastor and music director. A printed bulletin enables maximum participation.

If children of the couple(s) are present, they may participate by blessing the marriage, reading scripture lessons, singing or playing music, or making a witness in their own words.

GREETING

Friends, we are gathered together in the sight of God
to witness and bless
    the reaffirmation of the marriage covenant,
    which was established by God,
    who created us male and female for each other.
With his presence and power
    Jesus graced a wedding at Cana of Galilee,
and in his sacrificial love
    gave us the example for the love of husband and wife.

REAFFIRMATION OF THE MARRIAGE COVENANT

*The couple(s) face each other, join hands, and speak directly to each
other, repeating the vows, phrase by phrase, after the pastor.*

Husband to wife (husbands to wives):

In the name of God, and with a thankful heart,
I once again declare that
I, *Name,* take you, *Name,* to be my wife,
    to have and to hold
    from this day forward,
    for better, for worse,
    for richer, for poorer,
    in sickness and in health,
    to love and to cherish,
    until we are parted by death.
This is my solemn vow.

Wife to husband (wives to husbands):

In the name of God, and with a thankful heart,
I once again declare that
I, *Name,* take you, *Name,* to be my husband,
    to have and to hold
    from this day forward,
    for better, for worse,
    for richer, for poorer,
    in sickness and in health,
    to love and to cherish,
    until we are parted by death.
This is my solemn vow.

CONGREGATIONAL RESPONSE

Let us pray.

Eternal God, Creator and preserver of all life,
    author of salvation, giver of all grace:
Bless and sanctify with your Holy Spirit
    Wife's Name **and** *Husband's Name, (those)*
    who have reaffirmed their marriage covenant.
Enable them to grow in love and peace
    with you and with each other all their days,
    that they may reach out
    in concern and service to the world;
through Jesus Christ our Lord. Amen.

BLESSING OF THE MARRIAGE(S)

Instead of, or in addition to, the following, the pastor may offer the
Prayer of Thanksgiving (26). On the occasion of a marriage anniver-
sary, the pastor and/or the couple may offer one or both of the marriage
anniversary prayers on 42.

O God, you have so consecrated
    the covenant of Christian marriage
    that in it is represented
    the covenant between Christ and his Church.
Send therefore your blessing upon *Name* and *Name (these*
    couples), that they may surely keep their marriage covenant,
    and so grow in love and godliness together
    that their *home(s)* may be *(a) haven(s)* of blessing and peace;
through Jesus Christ our Lord. **Amen.**

If this order takes place during regular congregational worship, the
couple(s) may be dismissed with the following blessing and the usual
order of worship followed for the remainder of the service.

God the Eternal keep you in love with each other,
    so that the peace of Christ may abide in your home.
Go to serve God and your neighbor in all that you do.

If this order is part of a special service and Holy Communion is not
to be celebrated, the service continues with the Lord's Prayer.

If Holy Communion is to be celebrated, the congregation turns to A
Service of Word and Table III in UMH 15 or one of the musical
settings (UMH 17-25), and the pastor follows the text on 25-29,
beginning with Taking the Bread and Cup. On a marriage anniver-
sary, this prayer may follow communion:

Lord, as we have gathered at the table of your Son,
    bless *Name* and *Name* on their wedding anniversary.
Watch over them in the coming years,

and bring them to the feast of eternal life.
Grant this through Christ our Lord. **Amen.**

*Whether or not Holy Communion is celebrated, the service may
conclude with a hymn and the Dismissal with Blessing and the Peace
(see 30).*

MARRIAGE ANNIVERSARY PRAYERS

*Marriage anniversaries present a prime opportunity for both Church
and family to proclaim the joys and blessing of Christian marriage. This
can happen in various ways.*

*A pastor may be invited to attend the family celebration and offer prayer,
and the couple themselves may offer a prayer of thanksgiving.*

*A couple may choose the occasion of their anniversary to reaffirm their
marriage covenant (see 39-41), during which the pastor may offer this
or another suitable prayer as a Blessing of the Marriage.*

Lord our God,
Bless *Name* and *Name.*
We thank you for their marriage,
 [for the children they have nurtured,]
 and for all the good they have done.
As you blessed the love of their youth,
 continue to bless their life together with gifts of peace and joy.
We ask this through our Lord Jesus Christ, your Son,
 who lives and reigns with you and the Holy Spirit,
 one God, for ever and ever. **Amen.**

*The couple may offer this or another suitable prayer following, or instead
of, the Blessing of the Marriage:*

O God, our heavenly Father,
 on this anniversary of our wedding
 we give you thanks for your past blessings,
 and for your continual mercies now.
We thank you that with the passing days
 you have increased and deepened our love for each other.
We praise you for all the joys of our home and family life.
Renew your blessings upon us now,
 as we renew our vows of love and loyalty;
and may your Holy Spirit strengthen us
 that we may ever remain steadfast in our faith and in your
 service;
through Jesus Christ our Lord. **Amen.**

SERVICES OF
DEATH AND RESURRECTION

A SERVICE OF DEATH AND RESURRECTION

This service is found in UMH 870-75. *It is a service of Christian worship suitable for funerals and memorial services. It should be held in the church if at all possible and at a time when members of the congregation can be present. If the service is to be held in a church and led by anyone other than the pastor of that congregation, it should be done at the invitation of that pastor. This service is intended for use with the body of the deceased present, but it can be adapted for use at memorial services or other occasions.*

Use of the term Service of Death and Resurrection *is not intended to discourage use of the more familiar terms*—funeral, burial of the dead, *or* memorial service. Funeral *is appropriate for a service with the body of the deceased present.* Burial of the Dead *is appropriate for a service where the remains of the deceased are buried.* Memorial Service *is appropriate when the body of the deceased is not present.* Service of Death and Resurrection *was selected as being appropriate to any of the wide variety of situations in which this service might be used. It expresses clearly the twofold nature of what is done: the facts of death and bereavement are honestly faced, and the gospel of resurrection is celebrated in the context of God's Baptismal Covenant with us in Christ.*

When circumstances make the service as it stands inappropriate, the pastor may make adaptations, using the alternative acts of worship on 63-70 and other available resources. Ethnic and cultural traditions are encouraged and may be incorporated into the service at the discretion of the pastor. The organist or person in charge of the music should be consulted and work with the family in all decisions on music selection.

Traditionally, pastors have not accepted an honorarium for this service when the deceased was a member of the parish.

The coffin may be covered with a pall (a large cloth with a cross and other Christian symbolism), an act whose meaning is declared by the words: "As in baptism *Name* put on Christ, so in Christ may *Name* be clothed with glory." *The same pall is used in a congregation for all funerals and is a witness that everyone is equal before the table of the Lord. For each service the pall should be clean and free of wrinkles, and flowers should never be placed on top of it. Alternatively, the coffin may be covered with a flag, or flowers may be placed on it.*

The service itself should be seen as a part of the larger ministry of the Church at death. At several times during this ministry acts of worship are especially appropriate.

1) In ministry with the dying, prayers and other acts of worship are crucial. See 70-71.

2) The pastor should be notified immediately upon the death of a member or constituent of the congregation. Prayer and other acts of worship are crucial with the bereaved at the time of death (see 71-72). The pastor may have an important role in notifying others of the death.

3) Plans for the service and all other ministries following a death should be made in consultation with the family and subject to the approval of the pastor. If the family requests that there be military, fraternal, or other rites in addition to the Service of Death and Resurrection, the pastor should plan carefully the sequence and interrelationship of these services so that the service is not interrupted with other rites, and so that its integrity is supported and not compromised.

4) Facing the body of the deceased and closing the coffin bring home to the mourners the reality of death and are times when the support of pastor and Christian community is important. A variety of supportive ministries by church, family, friends, and other organizations may take place between the time of death and the time of the service; see A Family Hour or Wake (72-73). Children should be invited to be present at all these services.

5) The Service of Death and Resurrection itself, commonly called the funeral or memorial service, brings into focus the whole ministry of the Church at death. It presupposes that the encounter with the body of the deceased and the closing of the coffin have already taken place, and for this reason the coffin remains closed throughout the service and thereafter.

6) The committal service is not found in UMH because the congregation cannot be expected to carry hymnals to the graveside, but it is found here following the Service of Death and Resurrection. The committal may take place immediately following the funeral, or it may be a separate service at another time and place.

7) Reentry into the community by the chief mourners following the service takes time and can be facilitated by the supportive ministry of the Church. If the service itself does not include Holy Communion, it is sometimes helpful for the pastor to take communion to the family, perhaps at the first visit following the service.

8) Continuing support of representatives of the community, including ministries of prayer and worship as appropriate, is essential in the long-term process by which those who mourn find healing.

9) *Recurring memorial acts and services are occasions both of healing and of celebration. Mourners are especially open to supportive ministries on such occasions as Christmas, holidays, birthdays, and anniversaries of marriage or of death. Celebration of All Saints and other annual memorial services can also be particularly helpful.*

10) *It is essential that ongoing congregational life in its totality be centered in the Christian gospel, which is a message of death and resurrection. The way in which persons deal with all death—past, present, and future—will depend upon how central this gospel has become in their lives.*

ENTRANCE

The congregation may participate by using A Service of Death and Resurrection in UMH 870.

GATHERING

The pastor may greet the family.

Music for worship may be offered while the people gather.

Hymns and songs of faith may be sung during the gathering. See suggestions under Eternal Life and Funerals and Memorial Services in UMH 940-42.

The coffin or urn may be carried into the place of worship in procession, in which case the pall may be placed on it outside the place of worship with these words:

Dying, Christ destroyed our death.
Rising, Christ restored our life.
Christ will come again in glory.
As in baptism *Name* put on Christ,
    so in Christ may *Name* be clothed with glory.
Here and now, dear friends, we are God's children.
What we shall be has not yet been revealed;
but we know that when he appears, we shall be like him,
    for we shall see him as he is.
Those who have this hope purify themselves
    as Christ is pure.

THE WORD OF GRACE

If the coffin or urn is carried into the place of worship in procession, the pastor may go before it speaking these words, the congregation standing. Or if the coffin or urn is already in place, the pastor speaks these or other words (see 63, 64, 66, 68-69) from in front of the congregation.

Jesus said, I am the resurrection and I am life.
Those who believe in me, even though they die, yet shall they
    live,
  and whoever lives and believes in me shall never die.
I am Alpha and Omega, the beginning and the end,
  the first and the last.
I died, and behold I am alive for evermore,
  and I hold the keys of hell and death.
Because I live, you shall live also.

GREETING

Friends, we have gathered here to praise God
  and to witness to our faith as we celebrate the life of *Name.*
We come together in grief, acknowledging our human loss.
May God grant us grace, that in pain we may find comfort,
  in sorrow hope, in death resurrection.

If there has been no procession, the pall may be placed at this time.

Whether or not the pall is placed at this time, the sentences printed above under Gathering may be used here if they were not used earlier.

HYMN OR SONG

See suggestions under Eternal Life and Funerals and Memorial Services in UMH 940-42.

PRAYER

One or more of the following or other prayers (see 64-70) may be offered, in unison if desired. Petition for God's help, thanksgiving for the communion of saints, confession of sin, and assurance of pardon are appropriate here.

The Lord be with you.
And also with you.
Let us pray.

O God, who gave us birth,
you are ever more ready to hear
  than we are to pray.
You know our needs before we ask,
  and our ignorance in asking.

Give to us now your grace,
  that as we shrink before the mystery of death,
  we may see the light of eternity.
Speak to us once more
  your solemn message of life and of death.
Help us to live as those who are prepared to die.
And when our days here are accomplished,
  enable us to die as those who go forth to live,
  so that living or dying, our life may be in you,
  and that nothing in life or in death will be able to separate
  us from your great love in Christ Jesus our Lord. Amen.

Eternal God,
we praise you for the great company of all those
  who have finished their course in faith
  and now rest from their labor.
We praise you for those dear to us
  whom we name in our hearts before you.
Especially we praise you for *Name,*
  whom you have graciously received into your presence.
To all of these, grant your peace.
Let perpetual light shine upon them;
and help us so to believe where we have not seen,
  that your presence may lead us through our years,
  and bring us at last with them
    into the joy of your home
    not made with hands but eternal in the heavens;
through Jesus Christ our Lord. Amen.

The following prayer of confession and pardon may also be used:

Holy God, before you our hearts are open
  and from you no secrets are hidden.
We bring to you now
  our shame and sorrow for our sins.
We have forgotten
  that our life is from you and unto you.
We have neither sought nor done your will.
We have not been truthful in our hearts,
  in our speech, in our lives.
We have not loved as we ought to love.
Help us and heal us,
  raising us from our sins into a better life,
  that we may end our days in peace,
  trusting in your kindness unto the end;

through Jesus Christ our Lord,
who lives and reigns with you
in the unity of the Holy Spirit,
one God, now and for ever. Amen.

Who is in a position to condemn?
Only Christ, Christ who died for us, who rose for us,
who reigns at God's right hand and prays for us.
Thanks be to God who gives us the victory
through our Lord Jesus Christ.

PSALM 130

*This or another version of Psalm 130 (UMH 515, 516, or 848) may
be sung or spoken:*

Out of the depths I cry unto thee, O Lord!
Lord, hear my cry.
Let thine ears be attentive
to the voice of my supplication.
If thou, Lord, should mark iniquities,
Lord, who could stand?
But there is forgiveness with thee,
that thou may be feared.
I wait for the Lord, my soul waits,
and in his word do I hope.
My soul waits for the Lord
more than those who watch for the morning.
O Israel, hope in the Lord!
For with the Lord is great mercy.
With him is plenteous redemption,
and he will redeem Israel from all their sins.   (RSV, ALT.)

PROCLAMATION AND RESPONSE

OLD TESTAMENT LESSON

One or both of the following or another lesson may be read:

Comfort, O comfort my people, says your God.
Speak tenderly to Jerusalem, and cry to her
that she has served her term, that her penalty is paid,
that she has received from the Lord's hand double for all her sins.
A voice cries out: "In the wilderness prepare the way of the
Lord,
make straight in the desert a highway for our God.
Every valley shall be lifted up,

and every mountain and hill be made low;
the uneven ground shall become level, and the rough places a plain.
Then the glory of the Lord shall be revealed,
   and all the people shall see it together,
   for the mouth of the Lord has spoken."
A voice says, "Cry out!"
   And I said, "What shall I cry?"
All people are grass, their constancy is like the flower of the field.
The grass withers, the flower fades,
   when the breath of the Lord blows upon it;
surely the people are grass.
The grass withers, the flower fades;
   but the word of our God will stand forever.   (ISAIAH 40:1-8)

Have you not known? Have you not heard?
The Lord is an everlasting God, the Creator of the ends of the
   earth.
He does not faint or grow weary,
   his understanding is unsearchable.
He gives power to the faint, and strengthens the powerless.
Even youths will faint and be weary,
   and the young will fall exhausted;
but those who wait for the Lord shall renew their strength,
   they shall mount up with wings like eagles,
   they shall run and not be weary,
   they shall walk and not faint.   (ISAIAH 40:28-31)

Other Suggested Scripture Readings

Exodus 14:5-14, 19-31	Israel's deliverance
Isaiah 43:1-3*a*, 5-7, 13,	
15, 18-19, 25; 44:6, 8*a*	God will deliver.
Isaiah 55:1-3, 6-13	Hymn of joy

See Canticle of Covenant Faithfulness (UMH 125).

PSALM 23

*This or another version of Psalm 23 (UMH 136, 137, 138, or 754)
may be sung or spoken:*

**The Lord is my shepherd; I shall not want.
He maketh me to lie down in green pastures:
   he leadeth me beside the still waters.
He restoreth my soul:
   he leadeth me in the paths of righteousness
   for his name's sake.**

Yea, though I walk
 through the valley of the shadow of death,
  I will fear no evil:
for thou art with me;
 thy rod and thy staff they comfort me.
Thou preparest a table before me
 in the presence of mine enemies:
thou anointest my head with oil;
 my cup runneth over.
Surely goodness and mercy shall follow me
 all the days of my life:
  and I will dwell in the house of the Lord for ever.   (KJV)

NEW TESTAMENT LESSON

One of the following or another lesson may be read:

Now I would remind you, brothers and sisters,
of the good news that I proclaimed to you,
 which you in turn received, in which also you stand,
 through which also you are being saved.
Now if Christ is proclaimed as raised from the dead,
 how can some of you say there is no resurrection of the dead?
For if the dead are not raised, then Christ has not been raised.
If Christ has not been raised,
 your faith is futile and you are still in your sins.
Then those also who have died in Christ have perished.
But in fact Christ has been raised from the dead,
 the first fruits of those who have died.
But someone will ask, "How are the dead raised?
 With what kind of body do they come?"
Fool! What you sow does not come to life unless it dies.
And as for what you sow, you do not sow the body that is to be,
 but a bare seed, perhaps of wheat or of some other grain.
But God gives it a body as he has chosen.
What is sown is perishable, what is raised is imperishable.
It is sown in dishonor, it is raised in glory.
It is sown in weakness, it is raised in power.
It is sown a physical body, it is raised a spiritual body.
If there is a physical body, there is also a spiritual body.
When this perishable body puts on imperishability,
 and this mortal body puts on immortality,
then the saying that is written will be fulfilled:
"Death has been swallowed up in victory."

"Where, O death, is your victory? Where, O death, is your
sting?"
But thanks be to God,
who gives us the victory through our Lord Jesus Christ.
(1 CORINTHIANS 15:1-2*a*, 12, 16-18, 20, 35-38*a*, 42*b*-44, 54-55, 57)

Then I saw a new heaven and a new earth;
for the first heaven and the first earth had passed away,
and the sea was no more.
And I saw the holy city, the new Jerusalem,
coming down out of heaven from God,
prepared as a bride adorned for her husband.
And I heard a loud voice from the throne saying,
"See, the home of God is among mortals.
He will dwell with them as their God;
they will be his peoples, and God himself will be with them;
he will wipe away every tear from their eyes.
Death will be no more;
mourning and crying and pain will be no more,
for the first things have passed away."
And the one who was seated on the throne said,
"See, I am making all things new."
Also he said, "Write this, for these words are trustworthy and
true."
Then he said to me,
"It is done! I am the Alpha and the Omega,
the beginning and the end.
To the thirsty I will give water
as a gift from the spring of the water of life.
Those who conquer will inherit these things,
and I will be their God and they will be my children."
(REVELATION 21:1-7)

There is therefore now no condemnation
for those who are in Christ Jesus.
For the law of the Spirit of life in Christ Jesus
has set you free from the law of sin and of death.
If the Spirit of him who raised Jesus from the dead dwells in you,
he who raised Christ from the dead
will give life to your mortal bodies also
through his Spirit that dwells in you.
For all who are led by the Spirit of God are children of God,
and if children, then heirs,
heirs of God and joint heirs with Christ—

if, in fact, we suffer with him
  so that we may also be glorified with him.
I consider that the sufferings of this present time
  are not worth comparing
    with the glory about to be revealed to us.
We know that all things work together for good
  for those who love God,
  who are called according to his purpose.
What then are we to say about these things?
If God is for us, who is against us?
He who did not withhold his own Son,
  but gave him up for all of us,
  will he not with him also give us everything else?
Who will separate us from the love of Christ?
Will hardship, or distress, or persecution,
  or famine, or nakedness, or peril, or sword?
As it is written, "For your sake we are being killed all day long;
  we are accounted as sheep to be slaughtered."
No, in all these things we are more than conquerors
  through him who loved us.
For I am convinced that neither death, nor life,
  nor angels, nor rulers, nor things present, nor things to come,
  nor powers, nor height, nor depth, nor anything else in all
    creation,
  will be able to separate us from the love of God
  in Christ Jesus our Lord.
                    (ROMANS 8:1-2, 11, 14, 17-18, 28, 31-32, 35-39)

Other Suggested Scripture Readings

2 Corinthians 4:5-18	Glory in God
Ephesians 1:15-23; 2:1-10	Alive in Christ
1 Peter 1:3-9, 13, 21-25	Blessed by God
Revelation 7:2-3, 9-17	The multitude of the redeemed

PSALM, CANTICLE, OR HYMN

Recommended, either here or after the Old Testament Lesson:

Psalm 42 (*UMH 777*)	As a deer longs for flowing streams
Psalm 43 (*UMH 778*)	You are the God in whom I take refuge.
Psalm 46 (*UMH 780*)	God is our refuge and strength.
Psalm 90 (*UMH 809*)	From everlasting to everlasting
Psalm 91 (*UMH 810*)	My God in whom I trust
Psalm 103 (*UMH 824*)	Bless the Lord, O my soul.
Psalm 116 (*UMH 837*)	I will lift up the cup of salvation.
Psalm 121 (*UMH 844*)	I will lift up my eyes to the hills.

Psalm 139 (*UMH* 854)	O Lord, you have searched me.
Psalm 145 (*UMH* 857)	The Lord is gracious and merciful.
Psalm 146 (*UMH* 858)	Praise the Lord, O my soul.
Canticle of Hope (*UMH* 734)	God shall wipe away all our tears.
Canticle of Remembrance (*UMH* 652)	The souls of the righteous

See hymns suggested under Eternal Life and Funerals and Memorial Services in UMH 940-42.

GOSPEL LESSON

The following or another lesson may be read:

[Jesus said,] "Do not let your hearts be troubled.
Believe in God, believe also in me.
In my Father's house there are many dwelling places.
If it were not so,
   would I have told you that I go to prepare a place for you?
And if I go and prepare a place for you,
  I will come again and will take you to myself,
    so that where I am, there you may be also.
And you know the way to the place where I am going.
I will not leave you orphaned; I am coming to you.
In a little while the world will no longer see me,
  but you will see me;
  because I live, you also will live.
I have said these things to you while I am still with you.
But the Advocate, the Holy Spirit,
  whom the Father will send in my name,
  will teach you everything,
    and remind you of all that I have said to you.
Peace I leave with you; my peace I give to you.
I do not give to you as the world gives.
Do not let your hearts be troubled, and do not let them be
  afraid." (JOHN 14:1-4, 18-19, 25-27)

Other Suggested Scripture Readings

Luke 24:13-35	Jesus at Emmaus
John 11:1-4, 20-27, 32-35, 38-44	The raising of Lazarus

SERMON

A sermon may be preached, proclaiming the gospel in the face of death. It may lead into, or include, the following acts of naming and witness.

NAMING

The life and death of the deceased may be gathered up in the reading of a memorial or appropriate statement, or in other ways, by the pastor or others.

WITNESS

Pastor, family, friends, and members of the congregation may briefly voice their thankfulness to God for the grace they have received in the life of the deceased and their Christian faith and joy.

A poem or other reading such as If Death My Friend and Me Divide (UMH 656) may be read as a witness.

Signs of faith, hope, and love may be exchanged.

HYMN OR SONG

See suggestions under Eternal Life and Funerals and Memorial Services in UMH 940-42.

CREED OR AFFIRMATION OF FAITH

See UMH 880-89. A hymn or musical response may either follow or precede the Creed or Affirmation of Faith.

COMMENDATION

If the Committal (60-63) is to conclude this service, it may be shortened and substituted for the Commendation.

PRAYERS

One or more of the following prayers may be offered, or other prayers may be used. They may take the form of a pastoral prayer, a series of shorter prayers, or a litany. Intercession, commendation of life, and thanksgiving are appropriate here.

God of us all, your love never ends.
When all else fails, you still are God.
We pray to you for one another in our need,
    and for all, anywhere, who mourn with us this day.
To those who doubt, give light;
    to those who are weak, strength;
    to all who have sinned, mercy;
    to all who sorrow, your peace.
Keep true in us
    the love with which we hold one another.

In all our ways we trust you.
And to you,
    with your Church on earth and in heaven,
    we offer honor and glory, now and for ever.   **Amen.**

O God, all that you have given us is yours.
As first you gave *Name* to us,
    now we give *Name* back to you.

Here the pastor, with others, standing near the coffin or urn, may lay hands on it, continuing:

Receive *Name* into the arms of your mercy.
Raise *Name* up with all your people.
Receive us also, and raise us into a new life.
Help us so to love and serve you in this world
    that we may enter into your joy in the world to come. **Amen.**

Into your hands, O merciful Savior,
    we commend your servant *Name*.
Acknowledge, we humbly beseech you,
    a sheep of your own fold,
    a lamb of your own flock,
    a sinner of your own redeeming.
Receive *Name* into the arms of your mercy,
    into the blessed rest of everlasting peace,
    and into the glorious company of the saints of light. **Amen.**

The pastor may administer Holy Communion to all present who wish to share at the Lord's table, the people using A Service of Word and Table III (UMH 15) or one of the musical settings (UMH 17-25) and the pastor using An Order for Holy Communion in 57-59 below. Otherwise, the service continues as follows:

PRAYER OF THANKSGIVING

God of love, we thank you
    for all with which you have blessed us
        even to this day:
for the gift of joy in days of health and strength
    and for the gifts of your abiding presence and promise
        in days of pain and grief.
We praise you for home and friends,
    and for our baptism and place in your Church
    with all who have faithfully lived and died.
Above all else we thank you for Jesus,
    who knew our griefs,

who died our death and rose for our sake,
and who lives and prays for us.
And as he taught us, so now we pray.

THE LORD'S PRAYER

*All pray the Lord's Prayer, using one of the forms in UMH 270-71,
894-96.*

HYMN

*This may be a recessional hymn. See suggestions under Eternal Life
and Funerals and Memorial Services in UMH 940-42.*

DISMISSAL WITH BLESSING

*The pastor, facing the people, may give one or more of the following,
or other, Dismissal with Blessing:*

Now may the God of peace
who brought back from the dead our Lord Jesus,
the great Shepherd of the sheep,
by the blood of the eternal covenant,
make you complete in everything good
so that you may do his will,
working among us that which is pleasing in his sight,
through Jesus Christ;
to whom be the glory for ever and ever. **Amen.**

(HEBREWS 13:20-21)

The peace of God which passes all understanding
keep your hearts and minds in the knowledge and love of
God,
and of his Son Jesus Christ our Lord.
And the blessing of God Almighty,
the Father, Son, and Holy Spirit,
be among you and remain with you always. **Amen.**

Now may the Father
from whom every family in heaven and on earth is named,
according to the riches of God's glory,
grant you to be strengthened with might
through God's Spirit in your inner being,
that Christ may dwell in your hearts through faith;
that you, being rooted and grounded in love,
may be able to comprehend with all the saints
what is the breadth and length and height and depth,

and to know the love of Christ which surpasses knowledge,
that you may be filled with all the fullness of God. **Amen.**
(EPHESIANS 3:14-19, PARAPHRASE)

A Service of Committal follows at the final resting place. See 60-63.

AN ORDER FOR HOLY COMMUNION

*This order may be included in the Service of Death and Resurrection at
the point indicated on 55, or before a common meal following the service,
or with the family at some time following the service. The people use A
Service of Word and Table III (UMH 15) or one of the musical settings
(UMH 17-25). It is our tradition to invite all Christians to the Lord's
table, and the invitation should be extended to everyone present; but
there should be no pressure that would embarrass those who for
whatever reason do not choose to receive Holy Communion.*

TAKING THE BREAD AND CUP

*The pastor, standing if possible behind the Lord's table, facing the
people from this time through Breaking the Bread, takes the bread and
cup; and the bread and wine are prepared for the meal.*

THE GREAT THANKSGIVING

The Lord be with you.
And also with you.
Lift up your hearts. *The pastor may lift hands and keep them raised.*
We lift them up to the Lord.
Let us give thanks to the Lord our God.
It is right to give our thanks and praise.

It is right,
that we should always and everywhere give thanks to you,
Father Almighty *(almighty God),* Creator of heaven and earth;
through Jesus Christ our Lord,
who rose victorious from the dead
and comforts us with the blessed hope of everlasting life.

And so, with your people on earth and all the company of
heaven
we praise your name and join their unending hymn:

The pastor may lower hands.

**Holy, holy, holy Lord, God of power and might,
heaven and earth are full of your glory. Hosanna in the highest!
Blessed is he who comes in the name of the Lord.**

Hosanna in the highest!

The pastor may raise hands.

Holy are you, and blessed is your Son Jesus Christ.
By the baptism of his suffering, death, and resurrection
   you gave birth to your Church,
      delivered us from slavery to sin and death,
      and made with us a new covenant by water and the Spirit.
When the Lord Jesus ascended, he promised to be with us always
   in the power of your Word and Holy Spirit.

*The pastor may hold hands, palms down, over the bread, or touch the
bread, or lift the bread.*

On the night in which he gave himself up for us, he took bread,
   gave thanks to you, broke the bread, gave it to his disciples,
   and said: "Take, eat; this is my body which is given for you.
Do this in remembrance of me."

*The pastor may hold hands, palms down, over the cup, or touch the
cup, or lift the cup.*

When the supper was over he took the cup,
   gave thanks to you, gave it to his disciples, and said:
"Drink from this, all of you; this is my blood of the new
      covenant,
   poured out for you and for many
      for the forgiveness of sins.
Do this, as often as you drink it, in remembrance of me."

The pastor may raise hands.

And so, in remembrance of these your mighty acts in Jesus
Christ, we offer ourselves in praise and thanksgiving
   as a holy and living sacrifice,
   in union with Christ's offering for us,
as we proclaim the mystery of faith:

Christ has died; Christ is risen; Christ will come again.

The pastor may hold hands, palms down, over the bread and cup.

Pour out your Holy Spirit on us, gathered here,
   and on these gifts of bread and wine.
Make them be for us the body and blood of Christ,
that we may be for the world the body of Christ,
   redeemed by his blood.

The pastor may raise hands.

By your Spirit make us one with Christ,

one with each other, and one in communion with all your
    saints,
especially *Name* and all those most dear to us,
whom we now remember in the silence of our hearts.

A time of silence for remembrance.

Finally, by your grace, bring them and all of us to that table
    where your saints feast for ever in your heavenly home.

Through your Son Jesus Christ,
    with the Holy Spirit in your holy Church,
all honor and glory is yours, almighty Father *(God)*,
    now and for ever. **Amen.**

THE LORD'S PRAYER

The pastor's hands may be extended in open invitation.

And now, with the confidence of children of God, let us pray:

The pastor may raise hands:
All pray the Lord's Prayer, using one of the forms in UMH 270-71,
894-96.

BREAKING THE BREAD

The pastor, still standing behind the Lord's table facing the people,
breaks the bread and then lifts the cup, in silence or with appropriate
words.

GIVING THE BREAD AND CUP

The bread and wine are given to the people, with these or other words
being exchanged:

The body of Christ, given for you. **Amen.**
The blood of Christ, given for you. **Amen.**

While the bread and cup are given, the congregation may sing hymns,
or there may be vocal or instrumental music. In addition to the
suggestions under Eternal Life, Funerals and Memorial Services, and
Holy Communion in UMH 940-43, many other hymns in UMH are
effective in expressing the people's loving communion with God and
with one another. It is particularly effective if the people can sing from
memory during communion.

When all have received, the Lord's table is put in order.

DISMISSAL WITH BLESSING

The pastor, facing the people, may give one or more of the Dismissals with Blessing in 56, or another Dismissal with Blessing.

A Service of Committal follows at the final resting place. See below.

A SERVICE OF COMMITTAL

This order is intended primarily for burial in the ground. However, it can be adapted for cremation or the interment of ashes, for burial above ground or at sea, or for donation of the body for medical purposes.

If the family requests that there be military, fraternal, or other rites in addition to the Service of Committal, the pastor should approve such rites and plan carefully the sequence and interrelationship of these services so that the service is not interrupted.

The pastor will preside.

Prayers and lessons appropriate for a service for a child or youth, or for other distinctive occasions, may be used instead of the following. See 63-70.

When the people have gathered, one or more of the following are said:

In the midst of life, we are in death;
   from whom can we seek help? (NINTH CENTURY)

Our help is in the name of the Lord
   who made heaven and earth. (PSALM 124:8, *UMH* 846)

God who raised Christ from the dead
   will give life to your mortal bodies also
   through the Spirit that dwells in you. (ROMANS 8:11, ALT.)

Listen, I will tell you a mystery!
We will not all die, but we will all be changed.
For this perishable body must put on imperishability,
   and this mortal body must put on immortality.
Then the saying that is written will be fulfilled:
   "Death has been swallowed up in victory."
   "Where, O death, is your victory? Where, O Death, is your
     sting?"
But thanks be to God,
   who gives us the victory through our Lord Jesus Christ.
               (1 CORINTHIANS 15:51, 53, 54*b*-55, 57)

Therefore my heart is glad, and my soul rejoices;
   my body also dwells secure.

You, [Lord,] show me the path of life;
   in your presence there is fullness of joy,
   in your right hand are pleasures forevermore.
                       (PSALM 16:9, 11, *UMH* 748)

The following prayer is offered:

Let us pray.

O God, you have ordered this wonderful world
   and know all things in earth and in heaven.
Give us such faith that by day and by night,
   at all times and in all places,
   we may without fear commit ourselves
      and those dear to us
      to your never-failing love,
      in this life and in the life to come. **Amen.**

One of the following or other scriptures may be read:

Blessed be the God and Father of our Lord Jesus Christ!
By his great mercy we have been born anew to a living hope
   through the resurrection of Jesus Christ from the dead,
and to an inheritance which is imperishable, undefiled and
     unfading,
   kept in heaven for you.
In this you rejoice, though now for a little while you suffer trials
   so that the genuineness of your faith may prove itself worthy
     at the revelation of Jesus Christ.
Without having seen him, yet you love him;
though you do not now see him,
   you believe in him and rejoice with unutterable and exalted joy.
As the harvest of your faith you reap the salvation of your souls.
              (ADAPTED FROM 1 PETER 1:3-9)

Jesus said: "Very truly, I tell you,
   unless a grain of wheat falls into the earth and dies,
   it remains just a single grain;
   but if it dies, it bears much fruit.
Those who love their life lose it,
   and those who hate their life in this world
     will keep it for eternal life.
Whoever serves me must follow me,
   and where I am, there will my servant be also.
Whoever serves me, the Father will honor."   (JOHN 12:24-26)

Standing at the head of the coffin and facing it (preferably casting earth upon it as it is lowered into the grave) the pastor says:

Almighty God,
    into your hands we commend your *son/daughter Name*,
    in sure and certain hope of resurrection to eternal life
    through Jesus Christ our Lord. **Amen.**

This body we commit to the ground
(to the elements, to its resting place),
    earth to earth, ashes to ashes, dust to dust. (TRADITIONAL)

Blessed are the dead who die in the Lord.
Yes, says the Spirit, they will rest from their labors
    for their deeds follow them. (REVELATION 14:13, ALT.)

One or more of the following or other prayers is offered:

Gracious God,
    we thank you for those we love but see no more.
Receive into your arms your servant *Name*,
    and grant that increasing in knowledge and love of you,
    he/she may go from strength to strength
        in service to your heavenly kingdom;
through Jesus Christ our Lord. **Amen.**

Almighty God,
    look with pity upon the sorrow of your servants,
    for whom we pray.
Amidst things they cannot understand,
    help them to trust in your care.
Bless them and keep them.
Make your face to shine upon them, and give them peace. **Amen.**
O Lord, support us all the day long of our troubled life,
    until the shadows lengthen and the evening comes,
        and the busy world is hushed,
        and the fever of life is over and our work is done.
Then in your mercy grant us a safe lodging,
    and a holy rest, and peace at the last;
through Jesus Christ our Lord. **Amen.**

Eternal God, you have shared with us the life of *Name*.
Before *he/she* was ours, *he/she* is yours.
For all that *Name* has given us to make us what we are,
    for that of *him/her* which lives and grows in each of us,
    and for *his/her* life that in your love will never end,
    we give you thanks.
As now we offer *Name* back into your arms,
    comfort us in our loneliness,
    strengthen us in our weakness,

and give us courage to face the future unafraid.
Draw those of us who remain in this life closer to one another,
  make us faithful to serve one another,
  and give us to know that peace and joy which is eternal life;
through Jesus Christ our Lord. **Amen.**

The Lord's Prayer may follow.

A hymn or song may be sung.

The pastor dismisses the people with the following or another blessing:

Now to the One who is able to keep you from falling,
  and to make you stand without blemish
    in the presence of God's glory with rejoicing,
to the only God our Savior, through Jesus Christ our Lord,
  be glory, majesty, power, and authority,
    before all time and now and forever. **Amen.** (JUDE 24-25, ALT.)

ADDITIONAL RESOURCES FOR SERVICES OF DEATH AND RESURRECTION

FOR GENERAL USE

Words of Grace and Sentences

The Lord is my light and my salvation;
  whom shall I fear?
The Lord is the stronghold of my life;
  of whom shall I be afraid?   (PSALM 27:1, *UMH* 758)

Blessed be the Lord,
  who has heard the voice of my supplications!
The Lord is my strength and shield,
  in whom my heart trusts.   (PSALM 28:6-7a, *UMH* 760)

The Lord is merciful and gracious,
  slow to anger and abounding in steadfast love.
As a father shows compassion to his children,
  so the Lord shows compassion to the faithful.
For the Lord knows our frame, and remembers that we are dust.
The steadfast love of the Lord is from everlasting to everlasting
  upon the faithful,
and the righteousness of the Lord to children's children.
                              (PSALM 103:8, 13-14, 17, *UMH* 824)

Prayers

O Jesus Christ our risen Lord, you have gone before us in death.
Grant us the assurance of your presence,
that we who are anxious and fearful in the face of death
may confidently face the future,
in the knowledge that you have prepared a place
for all who love you. **Amen.**

O God, giver of life and conqueror of death,
our help in every time of trouble,
we trust that you do not willingly grieve or afflict us.
Comfort us who mourn;
and give us grace, in the presence of death, to worship you,
that we may have sure hope of eternal life
and be enabled to put our whole trust in your goodness and
mercy;
through Jesus Christ our Lord. **Amen.**

Almighty God, our Father, from whom we come,
and to whom our spirits return:
You have been our dwelling place in all generations.
You are our refuge and strength, a very present help in trouble.
Grant us your blessing in this hour,
and enable us so to put our trust in you
that our spirits may grow calm and our hearts be comforted.
Lift our eyes beyond the shadows of earth,
and help us to see the light of eternity.
So may we find grace and strength for this and every time of need;
through Jesus Christ our Lord. **Amen.**

AT THE SERVICE FOR A CHILD

Words of Grace and Sentences

Jesus said:
"Truly I tell you, unless you change and become like children,
you will never enter the kingdom of heaven.
Whoever becomes humble like this child
is the greatest in the kingdom of heaven.
Take care that you do not despise one of these little ones;
for, I tell you, in heaven
their angels continually see the face of my Father in heaven.
So it is not the will of your Father in heaven
that one of these little ones should be lost."

(MATTHEW 18:3-4, 10, 14)

Jesus said: "Let the little children come to me,
   and do not stop them;
for it is to such as these
   that the kingdom of heaven belongs."   (MATTHEW 19:14)

And he took them up in his arms,
   laid his hands on them, and blessed them.   (MARK 10:16)

The Lamb at the center of the throne will be their shepherd,
   and he will guide them to springs of the water of life,
   and God will wipe away every tear from their eyes.
                                                      (REVELATION 7:17)

Friends, we have gathered to worship God and to witness
      to our faith
even as we mourn the death of this infant,
      the child of *Name* and *Name*.
We come together in grief, acknowledging our human loss.
May God search our hearts, that in pain we may find comfort,
   in sorrow hope, in death resurrection.

See also Psalm 103:8, 13-14, 17 (UMH 824-25).

Prayers

O God,
   whose dear Son took little children into his arms and
      blessed them:
Give us grace, we pray,
   to entrust this child to your never-failing love and care;
and bring us all to your eternal life;
through the same Jesus Christ our Lord. **Amen.**

O God, we pray that you will keep in your tender love
   the life of this child whom we hold in blessed memory.
Help us who continue here to serve you with constancy,
   trusting in your promise of eternal life, that hereafter
   we may be united with your blessed children in glory
      everlasting;
through Jesus Christ our Lord. **Amen.**

God our Father, your love gave us life, and your care never fails.
Yours is the beauty of childhood,
   and yours the light that shines in the face of age.
For all whom you have given to be dear to our hearts, we thank
      you,
   and especially for this child you have taken to yourself.

Into the arms of your love we give *his/her* soul,
remembering Jesus' words,
"Let the children come unto me,
   for of such is the kingdom of heaven."
To your love also we commend the sorrowing parents
   and family.
Show compassion to them as a father to his children;
   comfort them as a mother her little ones.
As their love follows their hearts' treasure,
   help them to trust that love they once have known is never lost,
   that the child taken from their sight lives for ever in your
      presence.
Into your hands we also give ourselves,
   our regret for whatever more we might have been or done,
   our need to trust you more and to pray,
   all our struggle for a better life.
Comfort us all.
Keep tender and true the love in which we hold one another.
Let not our longing for you ever cease.
May things unseen and eternal grow more real for us,
   more full of meaning,
   that in our living and dying you may be our peace. **Amen.**
O Lord, you keep little children in this present world,
   and hold them close to yourself in the life to come.
Receive in peace the soul of your child *Name*,
   for you have said, "Of such is my kingdom of heaven." **Amen.**

Scripture Readings

2 Samuel 12:16-23	David and the death of his child
Isaiah 65:17-25	An infant who lives but a few days
Lamentations 3:19-26, 31-33	Remember my affliction. God is good.
Joel 2:1, 12-13, 23-25*a*, 26-29	Your sons and daughters will see visions.
Psalm 103:6-18 (*UMH* 824)	As a father pities his children
Matthew 11:25-30	God revealed to infants
Matthew 18:1-5, 10-14	Children are greatest in God's kingdom.
Matthew 19:13-15	Let the children come to me.
(Also Mark 10:13-16;	
Luke 18:15-17)	
Mark 5:35-43	Jesus' raising of the ruler's daughter
(Also Matthew 9:18-19, 23-26)	

Suggested Hymns from UMH

141 Children of the Heavenly Father   191 Jesus Loves Me
707 Hymn of Promise

FOR AN UNTIMELY OR TRAGIC DEATH

Words of Grace and Sentences

Blessed be the God who consoles us in all our affliction,
so that we may be able to console those who are in any affliction
   with the consolation
   with which we ourselves are consoled by God.

(2 CORINTHIANS 1:3*a*, 4)

Cast your burden on the Lord, and God will sustain you.

(PSALM 55:22*a*, ALT.)

Prayers

Jesus our Friend, you wept at the grave of Lazarus,
   you know all our sorrows.
Behold our tears, and bind up the wounds of our hearts.
Through the mystery of pain,
   bring us into closer communion with you and with
      one another.
Raise us from death into life.
And grant, in your mercy, that with *Name*,
   who has passed within the veil,
   we may come to live, with you and with all whom we love,
   in our Father's home. **Amen.**

God of us all, we thank you for Christ's grace,
   through which we pray to you in this dark hour.
A life we love has been torn from us.
Expectations the years once held have vanished.
The mystery of death has stricken us.
O God, you know the lives we live and the deaths we die—
   woven so strangely of purpose and of chance,
      of reason and of the irrational,
   of strength and of frailty, of happiness and of pain.
Into your hands we commend the soul of *Name*.
No mortal life you have made is without eternal meaning.
No earthly fate is beyond your redeeming.
Through your grace
   that can do far more than we can think or imagine,
   fulfill in *Name* your purpose that reaches beyond time
      and death.
Lead *Name* from strength to strength,
   and fit *Name* for love and service in your kingdom.
Into your hands also we commit our lives.

You alone, God, make us to dwell in safety.
Whom, finally, have we on earth or in heaven but you?
Help us to know the measure of our days, and how frail we are.
Hold us in your keeping. Forgive us our sins.
Save our minds from despair and our hearts from fear.
And guard and guide us with your peace. **Amen.**

Everliving God, in Christ's resurrection
  you turned the disciples' despair into triumph,
    their sorrow into joy.
Give us faith to believe
  that every good that seems to be overcome by evil,
  and every love that seems to be buried in death,
  shall rise again to life eternal;
through Jesus Christ, who lives and reigns with you for ever
  more. **Amen.**

Almighty God, in your keeping there is shelter from the storm,
  and in your mercy there is comfort for the sorrows of life.
Hear now our prayer for those who mourn and are heavy laden.
Give to them strength to bear and do your will.
Lighten their darkness with your love.
Enable them to see beyond the things of this mortal world
  the promise of the eternal.
Help them to know that your care enfolds all your people,
  that you are our refuge and strength,
    and that underneath are your everlasting arms. **Amen.**

Scripture Readings

Lamentations 3:19-26, 31-33	Remember my affliction. God is good.
Psalm 103 (*UMH 824*)	Bless the Lord, who redeems from death.
Revelation 21:1-6; 22:1-5	God will wipe away every tear.

See Canticle of Hope (UMH 734)

Mark 4:35-41	Jesus' calming of the storm
Luke 15:11-32	The prodigal son
John 6:35-40	God's will that nothing be lost

Suggested Hymns from UMH

534 Be Still, My Soul
557 Blest Be the Tie That Binds
141 Children of the Heavenly Father
510 Come, Ye Disconsolate
129 Give to the Winds Thy Fears
128 He Leadeth Me: O Blessed Thought
528 Nearer, My God, to Thee
117 O God, Our Help in Ages Past
480 O Love That Wilt Not Let Me Go
474 Precious Lord, Take My Hand
356 Pues Si Vivimos (When We Are Living) (esp. for young adult)
308 Thine Be the Glory (especially for a middle adult)

707 Hymn of Promise   525 We'll Understand It Better
452 My Faith Looks Up to Thee   By and By

AT THE SERVICE FOR A PERSON
WHO DID NOT PROFESS THE CHRISTIAN FAITH

*If the faith of the deceased or of the mourners is such that the pastor
considers parts of the Service of Death and Resurrection inappropriate,
adaptations may be made with appropriate consultation so that no one's
integrity is violated. The acts of worship below may not be appropriate
for persons who were adherents of other religions.*

Words of Grace and Sentences

The eternal God is our dwelling place,
 and underneath are the everlasting arms.

(DEUTERONOMY   33:27 RSV, ALT.)

The Lord is near to the brokenhearted,
 and saves the crushed in spirit.   (PSALM 34:18, *UMH 770*)

The Lord heals the brokenhearted, and binds up their wounds.
Great is our Lord, and abundant in power,
 whose understanding is beyond measure.

(PSALM 147:3, 5, UMH 859)

Prayers

O God our Father, Creator of us all, giver and preserver
 of all life:
We confess to you our slowness to accept death
 as part of your plan for life.
We confess our reluctance to commit to you those whom
 we love.
Restore our faith
 that we may come to trust in your care and providence;
through Jesus Christ our Lord. **Amen.**

O Lord, from everlasting to everlasting you are God.
Look down upon our sorrowing hearts today, we humbly pray,
 and be gracious to us.
Help all who mourn to cast every care upon you, and find
 comfort;
through Jesus Christ our Lord. **Amen.**

Almighty God, the fountain of all life,
 our refuge and strength and our help in trouble:

Enable us, we pray, to put our trust in you,
    that we may obtain comfort,
    and find grace to help in this and every time of need;
through Jesus Christ our Lord. **Amen.**

Eternal God, you know all things in earth and heaven.
So fill our hearts with trust in you
    that, by night and by day, at all times and in all seasons,
    we may without fear commit those who are dear to us
    to your never-failing love, for this life and the life to come.
    Amen.

Almighty and everlasting God,
    you are always more ready to hear than we are to pray,
    to give more than we desire or deserve.
Pour out upon us your great mercy,
    forgiving those things of which our conscience is afraid,
    and giving us those good things we are not worthy to ask,
but through Jesus Christ our Lord. **Amen.**

Scripture Readings

Ecclesiastes 3:1-15	For everything there is a season.
Lamentations 3:1-9, 19-26	God's steadfast love
Psalm 39 (*UMH* 773)	Make me to know the measure of my days.
Romans 14:7-13	Why do you pass judgment?
Matthew 5:1-12	The Beatitudes
Matthew 25:31-46	As you did it to one of the least
Luke 20:27-39	God of the living, to whom all live

(Also Matthew 22:23-33; Mark 12:18-27)

Suggested Hymn from UMH

707 Hymn of Promise

MINISTRY WITH THE DYING

When death is near, the pastor should be notified so that the ministry of the Church may be extended.

Holy Communion may be administered, using A Service of Word and Table V (7-10).

The Baptismal Covenant may be reaffirmed, using portions of The Baptismal Covenant I (UMH 33-39) as may be appropriate.

The pastor, joined by others as they are able, may pray the Lord's Prayer or Psalm 23.

See also resources for Ministry with Persons with Life-threatening Illness (108-9).

The pastor may pray one or more of the following prayers:

Lord Jesus Christ, deliver your child *Name* from all evil
    and set *him/her* free from every bond;
that *he/she* may rest with all your saints
    in the joy of your eternal home, for ever and ever. **Amen.**

Gracious God, you are nearer than hands or feet,
    closer than breathing.
Sustain with your presence our *brother/sister Name.*
Help *him/her* now to trust in your goodness
    and claim your promise of life everlasting.
Cleanse *him/her* of all sin and remove all burdens.
Grant *him/her* the sure joy of your salvation,
through Jesus Christ our Lord. **Amen.**

When a life-support system is withdrawn:

O God, you are the Alpha and Omega, the beginning and the end.
You breathed into us the breath of life,
    and watched over us all our days.
Now, in time of death, we return *Name* to you,
    trusting in your steadfast love,
through Jesus Christ our Savior. **Amen.**

A commendation at the time of death, the pastor laying his/her hand on the head of the dying person:

Depart in peace, *brother/sister Name;*
    in the name of God the Father who created you;
    in the name of Christ who redeemed you;
    in the name of the Holy Spirit who sanctifies you.
May you rest in peace, and dwell for ever with the Lord.

MINISTRY IMMEDIATELY FOLLOWING DEATH

In ministering to the bereaved immediately following a death, the pastor may pray extemporaneously, or pray one or more of the prayers of commendation on 54-55, or the following:

Almighty God, our Creator and Redeemer,
you have given us our *brother/sister Name,*
    to know and to love in our pilgrimage on earth.
Uphold us now

as we entrust *him/her* to your boundless love and eternal care.
Assure us that not even death
can separate us from your infinite mercy.
Deal graciously with us who mourn,
that we may truly know your sure consolation
and learn to live in confident hope of the resurrection;
through your Son, Jesus Christ our Lord. **Amen.**

Out of the depths we cry to you, O Lord. Hear our voice.
We wait for you, O God. Our souls wait for you.
Give us now your word of hope.
We know your love is steadfast, always there when we need it.
Let us feel your presence now in our time of sorrow.
Help us to look to tomorrow to see hope beyond grief,
through Jesus Christ our Lord. **Amen.**

After the death of a child:

Loving God, as your son Jesus took children into his arms
and blessed them,
give us grace to entrust *Name* into your steadfast love,
through Jesus Christ our Savior. **Amen.**

After the birth of a stillborn child or the death of a newly born child:

Merciful God, you strengthen us by your power and wisdom.
Be gracious to *Name (and Name)* in *their (her)* grief
and surround *them (her)* with your unfailing love;
that *they (she)* may not be overwhelmed by *their (her)* loss
but have confidence in your goodness,
and courage to meet the days to come;
through Jesus Christ our Lord. **Amen.**

*See A Service of Death and Resurrection for a Stillborn Child (74-76)
and prayers in A Service of Hope After Loss of Pregnancy (103-6).*

A FAMILY HOUR OR WAKE

*It is appropriate for family and friends to gather for sharing and prayers
in the church, funeral home, or family home on the day or night before
the Service of Death and Resurrection.*

*This order out of an African American worship tradition may be used
for such occasions, or the service may be as informal as is desired. It may
be led by either clergy or laypersons. Acts of worship suggested for the
Service of Death and Resurrection may be included or substituted for
those below. The coffin may be open or closed, depending on the wishes
of the family.*

If the deceased is a member of a fraternal or other organization that customarily holds services for its deceased members, the one appointed by that organization may wish to conduct a special service according to its customs. Plans for such services should be made in consultation with the family and subject to the approval of the pastor.

GATHERING

Greetings and condolences may be exchanged with family and friends.

GREETINGS OR INTRODUCTORY REMARKS

The leader may open with a brief greeting or introductory statement on behalf of the church, family, and friends, such as:

Friends, we are gathered here
   to honor the memory of our departed friend and *brother/sister*,
   Name.

HYMN

If desired, one or more stanzas of a well-known hymn or song may be sung or recited.

PRAYER

The leader or some other designated person may pray an extemporaneous prayer, or the following or another prayer:

Gracious God,
as your Son wept with Mary and Martha at the tomb
   of Lazarus,
look with compassion on those who grieve [especially *Names*].

Silence may be kept.

Grant them the assurance of your presence now
   and faith in your eternal goodness,
that in them may be fulfilled the promise
   that those who mourn shall be comforted;
through Jesus Christ our Lord. **Amen.**

SCRIPTURE

One of the following, or another scripture (see 48-53), may be read:

Psalm 23 (*UMH* 754)	The Lord is my shepherd.
Psalm 27 (*UMH* 758)	The Lord is my light.
Psalm 90:1-6, 12, 16-17 (*UMH* 809)	From everlasting to everlasting
Psalm 121 (*UMH* 844)	I lift up my eyes to the hills.
John 14:1-10a, 15-21, 25-27	Do not let your hearts be troubled.

WITNESS

Family, friends, and members of the congregation may briefly voice their thankfulness to God for the grace they have received in the life of the deceased and their Christian faith and joy. Signs of faith, hope, and love may be exchanged.

CLOSING PRAYER OR BLESSING

The following or another prayer or blessing may be spoken or sung:

The Lord bless us and keep us.
The Lord make his face to shine upon us and be gracious to us.
The Lord lift up his countenance upon us and give us peace.
Amen.   (NUMBERS 6:24-26, ALT.)

A SERVICE OF DEATH AND RESURRECTION FOR A STILLBORN CHILD

In addition to, or instead of, the following acts of worship, other acts of worship from 64-66 or from A Service of Hope After Loss of Pregnancy (103-6) may be included.

THE WORD OF GRACE *See 64-65 or 103.*

GREETING

Friends, we have gathered here in our grief
  to praise God and witness to our faith.
We come together in grief,
  acknowledging our human loss of one so young.
[*He/She* has been given the name _____ by *his/her* parents,
  with the Church's blessing.]
May God grant us grace, that in pain we may find comfort,
  in sorrow hope, in death resurrection.

PRAYER

One or both of the following is suggested:

Almighty God, loving Parent of all your children,
  we come in sorrow that *Name* has been taken from us so soon.
Sometimes the burdens of life almost overwhelm us.
Yet we put our full trust in you,
  knowing that through your Son Jesus Christ
  you are with us always.
We take comfort that your loving arms
  surround us in our time of grief.

Be with *Name's* mother,
  who has carried *him/her* with love for so long.
We know you feel her disappointment and pain.
May her faith be renewed in the days ahead
  as she regains her strength.
Be with *Name's father and/or other family members.*
You know the heaviness of *his (their)* heart(s).
Pour out upon *them (her)* your gracious healing,
in the name of Jesus Christ, the great Physician, we pray.
Amen.

Blessed Jesus, lover of children,
  in lowliness of heart we cry to you for help.
Expecting the life of a child, we have witnessed *his/her* death.
Our despair is profound,
  and we know you weep with us in our loss.
Help us to hear your consoling voice,
  and give healing to our grief, merciful Savior. **Amen.**

In some circumstances a prayer of confession and pardon (see 47-48) may be appropriate. If the pastor feels this is the case, the issue should also be addressed in the sermon and in counseling.

SCRIPTURE

One or more of the following is suggested:

Psalm 23 (*UMH* 754)	The Lord is my shepherd.
Psalm 130 (*UMH* 848)	Out of the depths I cry to you.
2 Corinthians 1:3-7	God consoles us in all our affliction.
Matthew 11:28-30	Come to me, all who carry heavy burdens.

SERMON

PRAYER OF COMMENDATION

All-loving and caring God, Parent of us all,
  you know our grief in our loss,
  for you too suffered the death of your child.
Give us strength to go forward from this day,
  trusting, where we do not understand, that your love
    never ends.
When all else fails, you still are God.
We thank you for the life and hope
  that you give
  through the resurrection of your Son Jesus Christ.
We pray to you for one another in our need,

and for all, anywhere, who mourn with us this day.
To those who doubt, give light; to those who
    are weak, strength;
    to all who have sinned, mercy; to all who sorrow, your peace.
Keep true in us the love with which we hold one another.
And to you, with your Church on earth and in heaven,
    we offer honor and praise, now and for ever. **Amen.**

Here the pastor, with others, standing near the coffin or urn, may lay hands on it, continuing:

Receive *Name* into the arms of your mercy.
Receive us also, and raise us into a new life.
Help us so to love and serve you in this world
    that we may enter into your joy in the world to come. **Amen.**

The pastor may administer Holy Communion. See 57-59.

PRAYER OF THANKSGIVING *See 55.*

If the Committal is part of the service, it occurs at this point.

THE LORD'S PRAYER *See UMH 270-71, 894-96.*

DISMISSAL WITH BLESSING *See 56.*

A Service of Committal may follow at the final resting place. The service on 60-63 may be adapted in accord with the specific needs.

DAILY PRAISE AND PRAYER

AN ORDER FOR MORNING PRAISE
AND PRAYER

This service is for use by groups at dawn or as they begin their day in prayer. The service is most effective when morning sunlight is visible.

The people may participate by using An Order for Morning Praise and Prayer in UMH 876.

The congregation may be invited to stand for the entire service, except during the reading of Scripture and Silence, when used.

CALL TO PRAISE AND PRAYER

O Lord, open our lips.
And we shall declare your praise.   (PSALM 51:15, ALT.)

MORNING HYMN

A hymn appropriate to the morning may be sung. Suggested from UMH:

674-81 Morning Hymns
947 Hymns listed under Morning
   Prayer
173 Christ, Whose Glory Fills
   the Skies
64 Holy, Holy, Holy!

658 This Is the Day the Lord Hath
   Made
185 When Morning Gilds the Skies
  65 Santo! Santo! Santo!
657 This Is the Day

PRAYER OF THANKSGIVING

One of the following or other prayers of thanksgiving may be said by the leader or by all together:

New every morning is your love, great God of light,
   and all day long you are working for good in the world.
Stir up in us desire to serve you,
   to live peacefully with our neighbors,
   and to devote each day to your Son,
   our Savior, Jesus Christ the Lord. **Amen.**
     (PRESBYTERIAN WORSHIP BOOK, U.S.A., 20TH CENTURY)

Eternal God, hallowed be your name.
Early in the morning, before we begin our work,
   we praise your glory.
Renew our bodies as fresh as the morning flowers.

Open our inner eyes, as the sun casts new light upon the
    darkness.
Deliver us from all captivity.
Like the birds of the sky,
    give us wings of freedom to begin a new journey.
As a mighty stream running continuously,
    restore justice and freedom day by day.
We thank you for the gift of this morning,
    and a new day to work with you. **Amen.**

(MASAO TAKENAKA, JAPAN, 20TH CENTURY, ALT.)

*See also For a New Day (UMH 676), Listen, Lord (UMH 677), and
For Help for the Forthcoming Day (UMH 681).*

SCRIPTURE

*The following or other readings appropriate to the morning, or to the
day or season of the Christian year, or to the nature of the occasion,
may be used:*

Deuteronomy 6:4-7	The Shema
Isaiah 55:1-3	Invitation to abundant life
Psalm 51 (*UMH* 785)	Prayer for cleansing and pardon
Psalm 63 (*UMH* 788)	Comfort and assurance
Psalm 95 (*UMH* 814)	Call to worship and obedience
Romans 12:1-2	Be transformed by God.
John 1:1-5, 9-14	In the beginning was the Word.

SILENCE

*Silent meditation on the scripture that has been read. This may be
concluded with a short prayer, such as* Let our prayers be accept-
able to you, O God, our rock and our salvation. **Amen.**

SONG OF PRAISE

*The traditional morning Song of Praise is the Song of Zechariah
(UMH 208, 209). The following psalms and canticles, or other
scripture songs or hymns, may also be sung:*

Psalm 100 (*UMH* 821)	Canticle of Light and Darkness (*UMH* 205)
Psalm 148 (*UMH* 861)	Canticle of Moses and Miriam (*UMH* 135)
Psalm 150 (*UMH* 862)	Canticle of Praise to God (*UMH* 91)
Canticle of God's Glory (*UMH* 82, 83)	Canticle of Thanksgiving (*UMH* 74)
Canticle of the Holy Trinity (*UMH* 80)	

PRAYERS OF THE PEOPLE

The following or other litany of intercession may be prayed, during which any person may offer a brief prayer of intercession or petition.

After each prayer, the leader may conclude: Lord, in your mercy, *and all may respond:* **Hear our prayer.**

Or the leader may intone: Let Us Pray to the Lord (UMH 485), *and all respond singing:* **Lord, have mercy.**

Together, let us pray

for the people of this congregation . . .

for those who suffer and those in trouble . . .

for the concerns of this local community . . .

for the world, its peoples, and its leaders . . .

for the Church universal—
  its leaders, its members, and its mission . . .

in communion with the saints. . . .

Following these prayers, all may sing one of the following from UMH:

490 Hear Us, O God	491 Remember Me
488 Jesus, Remember Me	487 This Is Our Prayer
485 Let Us Pray to the Lord	

THE LORD'S PRAYER *Sung or spoken.*
  See UMH 270-71, 894-96.

BLESSING

The grace of the Lord Jesus Christ,
and the love of God,
and the communion of the Holy Spirit
be with you all. **Amen.**

THE PEACE *Signs of peace may be exchanged.*

AN ORDER FOR MIDDAY PRAISE AND PRAYER

This service is for use by groups in the middle of the day, possibly before a noon meal or following a morning meeting.

The congregation may be invited to stand for the entire service. The service is most effective when sunlight is visible.

CALL TO PRAISE AND PRAYER

Even youths will faint and be weary,
and the young will fall exhausted;
but those who wait for the Lord shall renew their strength,
they shall mount up with wings like eagles,
they shall run and not be weary,
they shall walk and not faint. (ISAIAH 40:30-31)

HYMN

A hymn for the midday may be sung. Suggested from UMH:

62 All Creatures of Our God and King
154 All Hail the Power of Jesus' Name
155 All Hail the Power of Jesus' Name
451 Be Thou My Vision
527 Do, Lord, Remember Me
404 Every Time I Feel the Spirit
465 Holy Spirit, Truth Divine
397 I Need Thee Every Hour
521 I Want Jesus to Walk with Me
494 Kum Ba Yah
402 Lord, I Want to Be a Christian

102 Now Thank We All Our God
119 O God in Heaven
480 O Love That Wilt Not Let Me Go
454 Open My Eyes, That I May See
96 Praise the Lord Who Reigns Above
492 Prayer Is the Soul's Sincere Desire
116 The God of Abraham Praise
601 Thy Word Is a Lamp
67 We, Thy People, Praise Thee
526 What a Friend We Have in Jesus

PRAYER OF THANKSGIVING

God of mercy, this midday moment of rest is your
welcome gift.
Bless the work we have begun, make good its defects,
and let us finish it in a way that pleases you.
Grant this through Christ our Lord. **Amen.**
(LITURGY OF THE HOURS, U.S.A., 20TH CENTURY)

SONG OF PRAISE

A scripture song or hymn may be sung. Suggested from UMH:

834 Psalm 113
844 Psalm 121
845 Psalm 122
846 Psalm 124

847 Psalm 126
74 Canticle of Thanksgiving
91 Canticle of Praise to God

PRAYERS OF THE PEOPLE

*The following or other litany of intercession may be prayed, during
which any person may offer a brief prayer of intercession or petition.*

After each prayer, the leader may conclude: Lord, in your mercy,
and all may respond: **Hear our prayer.**

Or the leader may intone: Let Us Pray to the Lord (UMH *485*), *and all respond singing:* **Lord, have mercy.**

Together, let us pray

for the people of this congregation . . .

for those who suffer and those in trouble . . .

for the concerns of this local community . . .

for the world, its peoples, and its leaders . . .

for the Church universal—
    its leaders, its members, and its mission . . .

in communion with the saints. . . .

Following these prayers, all may sing a response. Suggested from UMH:

490 Hear Us, O God   491 Remember Me
488 Jesus, Remember Me   487 This Is Our Prayer
485 Let Us Pray to the Lord

THE LORD'S PRAYER *Sung or spoken.*
  See UMH 270-71, 894-96.

BLESSING

The God of peace be with us.
Amen.

Let us bless the Lord.
Thanks be to God.

THE PEACE *Signs of peace may be exchanged.*

AN ORDER FOR EVENING PRAISE AND PRAYER

This service is for use by groups as they end their day in prayer, especially before or after an evening meeting.

The people may participate by using An Order for Evening Praise and Prayer in UMH 878.

The congregation may be invited to stand for the entire service, except during the reading of Scripture and Silence, when used.

PROCLAMATION OF THE LIGHT

A large unadorned candle may be lighted and lifted in the midst of the community. The following may be sung or spoken:

Light and peace in Jesus Christ.
Thanks be to God.

[SERVICE OF INCENSE]

Since the fourth century of the early church, the burning of incense has served as a devotional sign of prayer, based on Psalm 141. A stick of incense may be lighted, or pieces of incense may be dropped onto a lighted piece of charcoal. During this time, the following may be read:

I call upon you, O Lord; come quickly to me;
    give ear to my voice when I call to you.
Let my prayer be counted as incense before you,
    and the lifting up of my hands as an evening sacrifice.

(PSALM 141:1-2)

See also Psalm 134 (UMH 850).

EVENING HYMN *Suggested from UMH:*

682-93 Evening Hymns
941 Hymns listed under Evening Prayer
498 My Prayer Rises to Heaven
686 O Gladsome Light (traditional opening hymn for Evening Prayer)

PRAYER OF THANKSGIVING

One of the following or other prayers of thanksgiving may be said by the leader or by all together:

We praise and thank you, O God,
    for you are without beginning and without end.
Through Christ, you created the whole world;
    through Christ, you preserve it.
You made the day for the works of light
    and the night for the refreshment of our minds and bodies.
Keep us now in Christ; grant us a peaceful evening,
    a night free from sin; and bring us at last to eternal life.
Through Christ and in the Holy Spirit,
    we offer you all glory, honor, and worship,
    now and for ever. **Amen.**

(LITURGY OF EVENING PRAYER, SYRIA, 4TH CENTURY)

In the brightness of your Son we spend each day;
in the darkness of the night you light our way;

always you protect us with the umbrella of your love.
To you, God, be all praise and glory forever and forever. **Amen.**

(1985 CHRISTIAN CONFERENCE OF ASIA YOUTH)

*See also For Protection at Night (UMH 691) and For a Peaceful
Night (UMH 693).*

SCRIPTURE

*The following or other readings appropriate to the evening, or to the
day or season of the Christian year, or to the nature of the occasion,
may be used:*

Genesis 1:1-5, 14-19	The creation
Exodus 13:21-22	Pillar of cloud and pillar of fire
Psalm 23 (*UMH* 137, 754)	The divine shepherd
Psalm 90 (*UMH* 809)	God's eternity and human frailty
Psalm 121 (*UMH* 844)	Song of praise and prayer
Romans 5:6-11	Christ died for the ungodly.
1 Thessalonians 5:2-10	The day of the Lord
Revelation 22:1-5	The city of God
Matthew 25:1-13	Parable of ten bridesmaids

SILENCE

*Silent meditation on the scripture that has been read. This may be
concluded with a short prayer.*

SONG OF PRAISE

*The traditional evening Song of Praise is the Song of Mary (UMH
198, 199, 200, 197 [stanza 4]). The following psalms and canticles,
or other scripture songs or hymns, may also be sung:*

Psalm 134 (*UMH* 850)	Canticle of Light and Darkness
Canticle of Hope (*UMH* 734)	(*UMH* 205)
Canticle of Covenant Faithfulness (*UMH* 125)	Canticle of Simeon (*UMH* 225)

PRAYERS OF THE PEOPLE

*The following or other litany of intercession may be prayed, during
which any person may offer a brief prayer of intercession or petition.*

After each prayer, the leader may conclude: Lord, in your mercy,
and all may respond: **Hear our prayer.**

Or the leader may intone: Let Us Pray to the Lord (UMH 485),
and all respond singing: **Lord, have mercy.**

Together, let us pray

for the people of this congregation . . .

for those who suffer and those in trouble . . .

for the concerns of this local community . . .

for the world, its peoples, and its leaders . . .

for the Church universal—
  its leaders, its members, and its mission . . .

in communion with the saints . . .

Or prayers of confession and words of pardon may be offered. See UMH *890-93.*

Following these prayers, all may sing a response such as one of the following from UMH:

490 Hear Us, O God   482 Lord, Have Mercy
483 Kyrie Eleison   491 Remember Me
484 Kyrie Eleison

THE LORD'S PRAYER *Sung or spoken.*
  See UMH *270-71, 894-96.*

BLESSING

The grace of Jesus Christ enfold you.
Go in peace.
Thanks be to God.

THE PEACE

Signs of peace may be exchanged, or all may depart in silence.

AN ORDER FOR NIGHT PRAISE AND PRAYER

This service of serenity and silence is for use by groups immediately prior to sleep or when retiring at night as they end their day in prayer. The people may remain seated for the entire service.

CALL TO PRAISE AND PRAYER

A large unadorned candle may be lighted. The following may be sung or spoken:

O God, come to our assistance.
O Lord, hasten to help us.

The Lord Almighty grant us a restful night and peace at the last.
Amen.

NIGHT HYMN *Sung or spoken. Suggested from* UMH:

682-93 Evening Hymns
941 Hymns listed under Evening Prayer
498 My Prayer Rises to Heaven
486 O Gladsome Light

PRAYERS OF CONFESSION

Prayers of confession and words of pardon may be offered. See UMH 890-93.

Following these prayers, all may sing. Suggested from UMH:

490 Hear Us, O God   484 Kyrie Eleison
482 Lord, Have Mercy   491 Remember Me
483 Kyrie Eleison

SILENCE

SONG OF PRAISE

The following or other scripture song or hymn from UMH *may be sung:*

741 Psalm 4   810 Psalm 91
767 Psalm 33   850 Psalm 134
769 Psalm 34   854 Psalm 139:1-12

SILENCE

PRAYER OF THANKSGIVING

One of the following or other prayers of thanksgiving may be said by the leader or by all together:

As you have made this day, O God,
  you also make the night.
Give light for our comfort.
Come upon us with quietness and still our souls
  that we may listen for the whisper of your Spirit
    and be sensitive to your nearness in our dreams.
Empower us to rise again in new life to proclaim your praise,
  and show Christ to the world. **Amen.**
(LITURGY OF THE HOURS, U.S.A., 20TH CENTURY)

Grant, O eternal God,
  that we may lie down in peace,
  and raise us up, O Sovereign, to life renewed.
Spread over us the shelter of your peace;
  guide us with your good counsel;
  and for your name's sake, be our Help.

Shield us from hatred and plague;
   keep us from war and famine and anguish;
   subdue our inclination to evil.
O God our Guardian and Helper,
   our gracious and merciful Ruler,
   give us refuge in the shadow of your wings.
O guard our coming and our going,
   that now and always we have life and peace.
Blessed is the Lord, Guardian of the people Israel for ever.
   Amen.

(JEWISH PRAYER FOR PROVIDENCE, U.S.A., 20TH CENTURY)

*See also: At the Close of Day (UMH 689), For Protection at Night
(UMH 691), and For a Peaceful Night (UMH 693).*

THE LORD'S PRAYER *Sung or spoken.*
   See UMH 270-71, 894-96.

COMMENDATIONS

In peace we will lie down and sleep.
In the Lord alone we safely rest.

Guide us waking, O Lord, and guard us sleeping,
**that awake we may watch with Christ,
   and asleep we may rest in peace.**

May the divine help remain with us always.
And with those who are absent from us.

(ORDER OF ST. LUKE, U.S.A., 20TH CENTURY, ALT.)

THE SONG OF SIMEON (*UMH* 225, 226)

BLESSING

May the God of hope
   fill you with all joy and peace in believing,
so that you may abound in hope
   by the power of the Holy Spirit.

(ROMANS 15:13)

THE PEACE

Signs of peace may be exchanged, and all may depart in silence.

OCCASIONAL SERVICES

AN ORDER OF THANKSGIVING
FOR THE BIRTH OR ADOPTION OF A CHILD

Following the birth or adoption of a child, the parent(s), together with other members of the family, may present the child in a service of worship to be welcomed by the congregation and to give thanks to God. Part or all of this order may be included in any service of congregational worship.

Thanksgiving for the birth or adoption of a child may also be offered to God in a hospital or home, using such parts of this order as are appropriate.

It should be made clear to participants that this act is neither an equivalent of nor a substitute for Holy Baptism but has an entirely different history and meaning. This act is appropriate (1) prior to the presentation of the child for baptism, or (2) if the child has been baptized elsewhere and is being presented for the first time in the congregation where his or her nurture is to take place.

While this order will not normally be the theme of an entire service, one or more of the following Scriptures may, if desired, be read as a lesson or sung as an act of praise and thanksgiving:

Deuteronomy 6:4-9	Diligently teach your children.
Deuteronomy 31:12-13	Do this that children may hear and learn.
1 Samuel 1:9-11, 19b-20, 26-28	Samuel born and lent to the Lord
Psalm 8 (*UMH* 743)	O Lord, how majestic is your name.
Galatians 4:4-7	We are God's adopted children.
Matthew 18:1-5	The greatest are humble like children.
Mark 10:13-16	Jesus blesses the children.
Luke 1:47-55 (*UMH* 198-200)	The Canticle of Mary
Luke 2:22-40	The presentation of Jesus in the Temple

As a Response to the Word or at some other appropriate place within a public worship service, the pastor invites those presenting children to come forward and then continues as follows:

PRESENTATION AND CALL TO THANKSGIVING

There may be informal and spontaneous acts of presentation and thanksgiving, and/or the following:

Brothers and sisters in Christ:
The *birth (adoption)* of a child is a joyous and solemn occasion

in the life of a family.
It is also an occasion for rejoicing in the church family.
I bid you, therefore, to join with *parent's Name* [and *parent's Name*]
  in giving thanks to God, whose children we all are,
  for the gift of *Child's Name* to be *their son/daughter*
[and with *sibling's Name(s)*, for a new *brother/sister*].

See also At the Birth of a Child (UMH 146).

PRAYER OF THANKSGIVING AND INTERCESSION

One or more of the following prayers is offered.

For the Birth of a Child

O God, as a mother comforts her children,
  you strengthen us in our solitude, sustain and provide for us.
As a father cares for his children,
  so continually look upon us with compassion and goodness.
We come before you with gratitude for the gift of this child,
  for the joy that has come into this family,
  and the grace with which you surround them and all of us.
Pour out your Spirit.
Enable your servants to abound in love,
  and establish our homes in holiness;
through Jesus Christ our Lord. **Amen.**

For a Safe Delivery

Gracious God, we give you humble and hearty thanks
  that you have preserved
    through the pain and anxiety of childbirth
  your servant *mother's Name*
  and upheld your servant(s) *Names of father and/or other family members.*
They desire (She desires) now to offer you
  their (her) praises and thanksgivings.
Grant in your mercy that by your help
  they (she) may live faithfully according to your will in this life,
  and finally partake of everlasting glory in the life to come;
through Jesus Christ our Lord. **Amen.**

For the Adoption of a Child

O God, you have adopted all of us as your children.
We give thanks to you for the child

who has come to bless *Name(s) of parent(s)*
[and *Name(s) of siblings*]
who have welcomed this child as *their* own.
By the power of your Holy Spirit,
fill their home with love, trust, and understanding;
through Jesus Christ our Lord. **Amen.**

For the Family

Gracious God,
from whom every family in heaven and on earth is named:
Out of the treasures of your glory,
strengthen us through your Spirit.
Help us joyfully to nurture *child's Name* within your Church.
Bring *him/her* by your grace to *baptism (Christian maturity)*,
that Christ may dwell in *his/her* heart through faith.
Give power to *child's Name* and to us,
that with all your people we may grasp
the breadth and length, the height and depth, of Christ's love.
Enable us to know this love,
and to be filled with your own fullness;
through Jesus Christ our Lord. **Amen.**

*A hymn or response may be sung and a blessing given. Suggested
from UMH:*

951 Listings under Doxology
186 Alleluia
53 All Praise to You
54 All Praise to You
611 Child of Blessing, Child of
  Promise (stanzas 2, 4)

141 Children of the Heavenly Father
92 For the Beauty of the Earth
  (stanzas 1, 4, 6)
72 Gloria, Gloria
78 Heleluyan
84 Thank You, Lord

A SERVICE FOR THE BLESSING OF A HOME

GATHERING *Family and friends gather inside or outside the
home.*

GREETING *The leader addresses the family and friends:*

Jesus said: "Listen! I am standing at the door, knocking;
if you hear my voice and open the door, I will come in."

Dear friends,
we have gathered together
to seek God's blessing upon this home,
which by the favor of God and human labor has been made
ready.

This home is not only a dwelling
    but a symbol to us of God's loving care
        and of our life together as the family of Christ.
Let us therefore bring praise and thanksgiving
    for goodness and mercy and for our communion,
offering ourselves as God's servants
    and as loving sisters and brothers to one another.

OPENING PRAYER

Let us pray.

Almighty and everlasting God,
    grant to this home the grace of your presence,
    that you may be known to inhabit this dwelling
        and defend this household;
    through Jesus Christ our Lord, who with you and the Holy
        Spirit lives and reigns, one God, for ever and ever. **Amen.**

SCRIPTURE *Suggested lessons:*

Joshua 24:14-15	As for me and my household, we will serve the Lord.
1 John 4:11-21	Those who abide in love abide in God.
Acts 2:43-47	Day by day . . . they broke bread at home.
Ephesians 3:14-21	Every family takes its name from God.
Matthew 6:25-33	Do not worry about your life.
Matthew 7:24-27	A house built on rock
John 14:1-3	In my Father's house are many dwellings.

CONSECRATION OF THE HOME

In the name of the Father, and of the Son, and of the Holy Spirit
(in the name of the holy and triune God),
    we consecrate this home,
    committing to God's love and care
        all (the one) who dwell(s) therein. **Amen.**

Let us pray.
Eternal God, bless this home.
Let your love rest upon it and your promised presence be
manifested in it.
May *the members of this household (Name)*
    grow in grace and in the knowledge of our Lord Jesus Christ.
Teach *them (him, her)* to love, as you have loved us;
and help us all to live in the peace of Jesus Christ our Lord.
Amen.

The service may conclude with the Lord's Prayer and Dismissal with Blessing or as indicated below.

CONSECRATION OF A PARSONAGE

This may be used in place of Consecration of the Home above.

In the name of the Father, and of the Son, and of the Holy Spirit
   (in the name of the holy and triune God),
      we consecrate this home for the pastors *(diaconal ministers)*
      and their families
      of *Name* United Methodist Church. **Amen.**

Let us pray.
Eternal God, bless this home provided as a parsonage
   to assure the domestic comfort of those called of God
      and appointed by the Bishop to serve this congregation.
May those who reside here
   experience the love and support of this congregation
      as very special persons in this family of God.
Help us love each other as you have loved us
   and help us all to live in the peace of Jesus Christ our Lord.
   Amen.

The service may conclude with the Lord's Prayer and Dismissal with Blessing or as indicated below.

SYMBOLIC ACTS

At this point symbolic expressions may be appropriate: the presentation of a gift such as a cross, painting, or other gift, or the planting of a tree or shrub. These actions may be accompanied by suitable blessings.

HOLY COMMUNION

It is appropriate to gather the people for a household celebration of Holy Communion, with the pastor presiding, using the dining table as the Lord's table and perhaps bread baked in the oven of the new home. See The Great Thanksgiving on 8-9 and hymn suggestions on UMH 943.

BLESSING

HEALING SERVICES
AND PRAYERS

INTRODUCTION

Scripture strongly affirms ministries of spiritual healing, which in recent years have received renewed emphasis throughout Christ's holy Church. The root of the word *healing* in New Testament Greek, *sozo*, is the same as that of *salvation* and *wholeness*. Spiritual healing is God's work of offering persons balance, harmony, and wholeness of body, mind, spirit, and relationships through confession, forgiveness, and reconciliation. Through such healing, God works to bring about reconciliation between God and humanity, among individuals and communities, within each person, and between humanity and the rest of creation. The New Testament records that Jesus himself healed the estranged and sick and sent out his disciples on ministries of healing. James (5:14-16a) calls us also to pray for and anoint the sick, that they may be healed.

All healing is of God. The Church's healing ministry in no way detracts from the gifts God gives through medicine and psychotherapy. It is no substitute for either medicine or the proper care of one's health. Rather, it adds to our total resources for wholeness.

Healing is not magic, but underlying it is the great mystery of God's love. Those who minister spiritual healing are channels of God's love. Although no one can predict what will happen in a given instance, many marvelous healings have taken place.

God does not promise that we shall be spared suffering but does promise to be with us in our suffering. Trusting that promise, we are enabled to recognize God's sustaining presence in pain, sickness, injury, and estrangement.

Likewise, God does not promise that we will be cured of all illnesses; and we all must face the inevitability of death. A Service of Healing is not necessarily a service of curing, but it provides an atmosphere in which healing can happen. The greatest healing of all is the reunion of reconciliation of a human being with God. When this happens, physical healing sometimes occurs, mental and emotional balance is often restored, spiritual health is enhanced, and relationships are healed. For the Christian the basic purpose of spiritual healing is to renew and strengthen one's relationship with the living Christ.

Patterns of healing services grow out of both Church traditions and the needs of the moment. Prayers for healing, accompanied if desired by anointing with the laying on of hands, may be incorporated into any service of congregational worship as a Response to the Word. Also, there may be a healing service at a stated time each week or month, or healing may be ministered privately to individuals. Many find not only prayer but also Holy Communion, laying on of hands, and anointing with oil to be healing.

Laying on of hands, anointing with oil, and the less formal gesture of holding someone's hand all show the power of touch, which plays a central role in the healings recorded in the New Testament. Jesus often touched others—blessing children, washing feet, healing injuries or disease, and raising people from death. Biblical precedent combines with our natural desire to reach out to persons in need in prompting us to touch gently and lovingly those who ask for healing prayers. Such an act is a tangible expression of the presence of the healing Christ, working in and through those who minister in his name.

Anointing the forehead with oil is a sign act invoking the healing love of God. The oil points beyond itself and those doing the anointing to the action of the Holy Spirit and the presence of the healing Christ, who is God's Anointed One. Olive oil is traditionally used in anointing but can become rancid. Sweet oil, which is olive oil with a preservative, is available in any pharmacy. Fragrant oils may be used, but care must be taken because some people are allergic to perfumes.

In addition to the general services of healing provided below, resources are included for special needs: for persons grieving after loss of pregnancy, for persons going through divorce, for a person suffering from addiction or substance abuse, for a person with AIDS, for a person with life-threatening illness, and for a person in a coma or unable to communicate. The suggested scriptures, prayers, and hymns may be used in a Service of Healing or on any suitable occasion. The prayers of confession in *UMH* 890-93 will be useful in many situations, particularly when there is a need for reconciliation (healing of relationships) with God, with other people, and with oneself. Also, the following prayers for healing are found in *UMH*:

466 An Invitation to Christ   461 For Those Who Mourn
458 Dear Lord, for All in Pain   460 In Time of Illness

(may be spoken or sung)   481 Prayer of Saint Francis
457 For the Sick   459 The Serenity Prayer

It is important that those ministering in services of healing be sensitive to the differences that exist among those who come for healing ministries. Sound preaching, teaching, and pastoral care are essential for healing ministries to accomplish their purpose.

A SERVICE OF HEALING I

This is a congregational service centered on healing and is for use at some time other than that of the principal weekly congregational worship service. It may be freely adapted to meet specific needs.

GATHERING

GREETING *One of the following may be used:*

Are any among you sick?
They should call for the elders of the church
   and have them pray over them,
   anointing them with oil in the name of the Lord.
The prayer of faith will save the sick,
   and the Lord will raise them up;
   and anyone who has committed sins will be forgiven.
Therefore confess your sins to one another,
   and pray for one another,
so that you may be healed.   (JAMES 5:14-16*a*)

May grace and peace be yours in abundance
   in the knowledge of God and of Jesus our Lord.   (2 PETER 1:2)
We have come to lift up our brothers and sisters before the Lord
   that they might receive healing.
Let those who seek God's healing
   open their hearts to the Spirit of the Lord.

Bless the Lord, O my soul!
And all that is within me, bless God's holy name!

Bless the Lord, O my soul, and forget not all God's benefits.
The Lord forgives all our iniquity, and heals all our diseases.

The Lord redeems our lives from the pit,
   and crowns us with steadfast love and mercy.
God satisfies us with good as long as we live
   so that our youth is renewed like the eagle's.

HYMN OF PRAISE

A hymn of adoration and praise (see UMH 57-152 and the listing in UMH 934) or one of the hymns of healing listed below on 100 may be sung.

OPENING PRAYER *The following or another prayer may be used.*
Almighty and everlasting God,
who can banish all affliction both of soul and of body,
show forth your power upon those in need,
that by your mercy they may be restored to serve you afresh
in holiness of living, through Jesus Christ our Lord. **Amen.**

SCRIPTURE *Suggested lessons and psalms:*

Ecclesiastes 3:1-11*a*	For everything there is a season.
Isaiah 26:3-4	Trust in the Lord forever.
Isaiah 35:1-10	Restoration of all that is broken
Isaiah 40:28-31	The weak shall renew their strength.
Isaiah 43:1-3*a*, 18-19, 25	When you pass through the waters
Isaiah 53:3-5	With his stripes we are healed.
Isaiah 61:1-3*a*	Good tidings to the afflicted
Psalm 13 (*UMH* 746)	A prayer of pain and sorrow
Psalm 23	You have anointed my head with oil.
	See *UMH* 128, 136, 137, 138, 518, 754.
Psalm 27 (*UMH* 758)	God is the strength of my life.
Psalm 30 (*UMH* 762)	Recovery from grave illness
Psalm 41 (*UMH* 776)	Assurance of God's help
Psalm 42 (*UMH* 777)	My soul longs for you.
Psalm 51:1-12, 15-17 (*UMH* 785)	Create in me a clean heart.
Psalm 91 (*UMH* 810)	Refuge under God's wings
Psalm 103 (*UMH* 824)	God forgives all your sins.
Psalm 130 (*UMH* 515, 516, 848)	Out of the depths
Psalm 138 (*UMH* 853)	Fulfill your purpose for me.
Psalm 139 (*UMH* 854)	The inescapable God
Psalm 146 (*UMH* 858)	God lifts the bowed down.
Acts 3:1-10	Peter and John heal the lame man.
Acts 5:12-16	Healings in Jerusalem
Romans 8	Nothing can separate us from God's love.
Romans 14:7-12	We live to the Lord.
2 Corinthians 1:3-5	God comforts us in affliction.
2 Corinthians 4:16-18	What can be seen is temporary.
Colossians 1:11-29	May you be strengthened with all power.
Hebrews 12:1-2	Jesus, the perfecter of our faith
James 5:13-16	Is any among you sick?
1 John 4:16*b*-19	There is no fear in love.
1 John 5:13-15	The confidence we have in Christ
Revelation 21:1-4	New heaven and new earth
Matthew 5:1-12	Blessed are they.

Matthew 8:1-13	The healing of a leper and servant
Matthew 10:1-8	Jesus sends the twelve disciples to heal.
Matthew 11:28-30	All who labor and are heavy laden
Matthew 15:21-28	The Canaanite woman's faith
Matthew 26:36-39	Not what I want, but what you want
Mark 1:21-28	Jesus heals a man with an unclean spirit.
Mark 5:1-20	My name is Legion, for we are many.
Mark 5:21-43	Girl restored to life, a woman healed
Mark 6:7-13	Anointing of the sick with oil
Mark 6:53-56	People brought the sick to Jesus.
Mark 8:22-26	A blind man at Bethsaida
Mark 10:46-52	Take heart; rise, Jesus is calling you.
Luke 5:17-26	Take up your pallet and walk.
Luke 7:11-17	Jesus raises the widow's son at Nain.
Luke 8:43-48	The woman with an issue of blood
Luke 17:11-19	Thanksgiving for healing
John 3:16-17	God so loved the world
John 5:2-18	Do you want to be healed?
John 9	Healing of the man born blind
John 11:1-44	Raising of Lazarus

SERMON, MEDITATION, OR TESTIMONY

[AFFIRMATION OF FAITH
OR OTHER RESPONSE TO THE WORD]

CONFESSION AND PARDON

If James 5:14-16a has not been read earlier in the service, it may be read as a call to confession.

The congregation may pray a confession such as one of those in UMH 890-93 or an appropriate psalm (see above).

The confession is followed by silence and these or other words of pardon.

Leader to people:

Hear the good news:
  Christ died for us while we were yet sinners;
  that proves God's love toward us.
In the name of Jesus Christ, you are forgiven!

People to leader:

In the name of Jesus Christ, you are forgiven.

Leader and people:

Glory to God. Amen.

The congregation may then sing a response of praise and thanksgiving such as one of the following from UMH:

162 Alleluia, Alleluia   78 Heleluyan
72 Gloria, Gloria   84 Thank You, Lord

[THE PEACE]

If desired, the Peace, Offering, and Holy Communion may follow the Anointing and Laying on of Hands.

[OFFERING]

[HOLY COMMUNION]

The pastor may administer Holy Communion to all present who wish to share at the Lord's table, the people using A Service of Word and Table III (UMH 15) or one of the musical settings (UMH 17-25) and the pastor using the following.

The pastor, standing if possible behind the Lord's table, facing the people from this time through the Breaking of Bread, takes the bread and cup; and the bread and wine are prepared for the meal. The pastor then prays:

The Lord be with you.
And also with you.
Lift up your hearts. *The pastor may lift hands and keep them raised.*
We lift them up to the Lord.
Let us give thanks to the Lord our God.
It is right to give our thanks and praise.

It is right, and a good and joyful thing,
   always and everywhere to give thanks to you,
      Father Almighty *(almighty God)*, creator of heaven and earth.
In the beginning, when darkness covered the face of the earth
   and nothing existed but chaos,
      your Spirit swept across the waters.
You spoke but a word, and light was separated from darkness.

And so, with your people on earth and all the company
      of heaven
   we praise your name and join their unending hymn:

The pastor may lower hands.

Holy, holy, holy Lord, God of power and might,
heaven and earth are full of your glory. Hosanna in the
   highest.

**Blessed is he who comes in the name of the Lord.
Hosanna in the highest.**

The pastor may raise hands.

Holy are you, and blessed is your Son Jesus Christ:
    who lived among us and knew human pain and suffering;
    who called all who were burdened and heavy laden
        and gave them rest;
    who healed the sick, fed the hungry, and ate with sinners;
    who cast out demons
        and showed us the way to you through faith;
    who took our suffering upon himself;
        that we might be cleansed of our sins and receive eternal life.
By the baptism of his suffering, death, and resurrection,
you gave birth to your Church,
    delivered us from slavery to sin and death,
    and made with us a new covenant by water and the Spirit.

*The pastor may hold hands, palms down, over the bread, or touch the
bread, or lift the bread.*

On the night in which he gave himself up for us, he took bread,
    gave thanks to you, broke the bread, gave it to his disciples,
        and said:
"Take, eat; this is my body which is given for you.
Do this in remembrance of me."

*The pastor may hold hands, palms down, over the cup, or touch the
cup, or lift the cup.*

When the supper was over he took the cup,
    gave thanks to you, gave it to his disciples, and said:
"Drink from this, all of you; this is my blood of the new
        covenant,
    poured out for you and for many for the
        forgiveness of sins.
    Do this, as often as you drink it, in remembrance of me."

The pastor may raise hands.

And so, in remembrance of these your mighty acts in
    Jesus Christ,
we offer ourselves in praise and thanksgiving
    as a holy and living sacrifice,
    in union with Christ's offering for us,
as we proclaim the mystery of faith:

Christ has died; Christ is risen; Christ will come again.

The pastor may hold hands, palms down, over the bread and cup.

Pour out your Holy Spirit on us gathered here,
   and on these gifts of bread and wine.
Make them be for us the body and blood of Christ,
   that we may be for the world the body of Christ,
   redeemed by his blood.

The pastor may raise hands.

By the same Spirit heal us in body, mind, and spirit,
   cleansing away all that would separate us from you.
By your Spirit make us one with Christ,
   one with each other, and one in ministry to all the world,
until Christ comes in victory, and we feast at his heavenly
   banquet.

Through your Son Jesus Christ,
   with the Holy Spirit in your holy Church,
all honor and glory is yours, almighty Father *(God)*,
   now and for ever.
Amen.

All pray the Lord's Prayer, using one of the forms in UMH 270-71,
894-96.

*The pastor, still standing behind the Lord's table, facing the people,
breaks the bread and then lifts the cup, in silence or with appropriate
words.*

*The bread and wine are given to the people, with these or other words
being exchanged:*

The body of Christ, given for you. **Amen.**
The blood of Christ, given for you. **Amen.**

When all have received, the Lord's table is put in order.

[THANKSGIVING OVER THE OIL]

If desired, this act may precede Holy Communion.

*If James 5:14-16a has not been read earlier in the service, it may be
read here as an introduction to the anointing.*

Let us pray.

O God, the giver of health and salvation,
   we give thanks to you for the gift of oil.
As your holy apostles anointed many who were sick
   and healed them,
so pour out your Holy Spirit on us and on this gift,

that those who in faith and repentance receive this anointing
may be made whole;
through Jesus Christ our Lord. **Amen.**

[HYMN OF HEALING]

*One of the hymns listed in UMH 943-44 under Healing or Hope or
in UMH 940 under Courage, or one of the following hymns in UMH,
or another suitable hymn may be sung by the congregation or by a
choir or solo voice.*

516 Canticle of Redemption
130 God Will Take Care of You
560 Help Us Accept Each Other
474 Precious Lord, Take My Hand

523 Saranam, Saranam
393 Spirit of the Living God
375 There Is a Balm in Gilead

PRAYERS FOR HEALING AND WHOLENESS WITH ANOINTING AND/OR LAYING ON OF HANDS

*People may be invited to come forward individually or as a group to
the communion rail or other designated prayer area and express any
specific concerns they may have. They may be ministered to by the
pastor, by other designated persons, or by prayer teams of two or three
persons each. All prayer team members lay on hands and share in
silent and spoken prayer.*

*The congregation and choir may sing hymns. See hymns suggested
above.*

*If there is anointing with oil, a leader touches a thumb to the oil and
makes the sign of the cross on the person's forehead, in silence or using
these or similar words:*

Name, I anoint you with oil
in the name of the Father, and of the Son, and of the Holy Spirit
(in the name of the holy and triune God)
(in the name of Jesus, the Christ, your Savior and Healer)
[for *specified purpose*].

*If there is laying on of hands, a leader, who may be joined by others,
lays hands upon each person's head, in silence or using these or
similar words:*

Name, I *(we)* lay my *(our)* hands on you
(These hands are laid upon you)
in the name of the Father, and of the Son, and of the Holy Spirit
(in the name of the holy and triune God)
(in the name of Jesus, the Christ, your Savior and Healer)
[for *specified purpose*].

May the power of God's indwelling presence
  heal you of all illnesses—
  of body, mind, spirit, and relationships—
that you may serve God with a loving heart. **Amen.**

PRAYER AFTER ANOINTING
AND/OR LAYING ON OF HANDS

*The following, or one of the prayers for special concerns on 106-9, or
another suitable prayer may be used.*

Almighty God,
  we pray that *Names (our brothers and sisters)*
    may be comforted in their suffering and made whole.
When they are afraid, give them courage;
when they feel weak, grant them your strength;
when they are afflicted, afford them patience;
when they are lost, offer them hope;
when they are alone, move us to their side;
[when death comes, open your arms to receive *him/her*].
In the name of Jesus Christ we pray. **Amen.**

[SHARING OF THANKSGIVINGS]

Persons who feel so led may give thanks for healing or other blessings.

HYMN *One of the hymns suggested above or another suitable
  hymn.*

DISMISSAL WITH BLESSING

The Lord who heals all your iniquity bless and keep you;
the face of the Lord who heals all your afflictions
  shine upon you and be gracious to you;
the light of the countenance of the Lord who redeems your life
  be lifted upon you and give you peace. **Amen.**

GOING FORTH

A SERVICE OF HEALING II

*This service may be used in private or in corporate worship. It may take
place in a church, home, or hospital, or at a meeting of a prayer group.
The service may be adapted for special needs by selecting appropriate
portions from it and from any of the additional resources on 106-9.
Hymns suggested in A Service of Healing I may also be used.*

GREETING AND PREPARATION

SCRIPTURE *See lessons suggested above (95-96).*

Comments on the lesson(s) may be added as appropriate.

CONFESSION AND PARDON

If it seems appropriate, the person(s) present may be invited to share any trouble or difficulty that hinders his or her relationship with God, using one of the following or another suitable invitation:

Name, the Scriptures tell us to bear one another's burdens
  and so fulfill the law of Christ.
As your *sister/brother* in Christ, I ask you now,
are you at peace with God,
or is there anything in your life
  that causes you to feel separated from God
    and less than the full person God calls you to be?

Name, the Scriptures tell us not to be anxious about our lives
  or about tomorrow.
Are there anxieties
  that cause you to feel separated from the peace that God
    promises?

There may be silence, reflection, or personal sharing.

A Confession and Pardon from A Service of Word and Table V (7-10) or UMH 890-93, or an appropriate psalm (see 95) may be used.

[HOLY COMMUNION]

The pastor may administer Holy Communion, using A Service of Word and Table V on 7-10.

PRAYERS FOR HEALING AND WHOLENESS WITH ANOINTING AND/OR LAYING ON OF HANDS

If there is anointing with oil, a leader touches a thumb to the oil and makes the sign of the cross on the person's forehead, in silence or using these or similar words:

Name, I anoint you with oil
  in the name of the Father, and of the Son, and of the Holy Spirit
  (in the name of the holy and triune God)
[for *specified purpose*].
If there is laying on of hands, a leader, who may be joined by others, lays hands upon each person's head, in silence or using these or similar words:

Name, I *(we)* lay my *(our)* hands on you
in the name of the Father, and of the Son, and of the Holy Spirit
  (in the name of the holy and triune God)
[for *specified purpose*].

PRAYERS OF INTERCESSION

*One of the prayers for special concerns on 106-9, or another suitable
prayer.*

THE LORD'S PRAYER

BLESSING

A SERVICE OF HOPE AFTER LOSS
OF PREGNANCY

*This service may be held in a church, hospital, or home. Any of the
scriptures and prayers may also be used by themselves.*

*Any of the acts of worship suggested at the death of a child (64-66) or
in A Service of Death and Resurrection for a Stillborn Child (74-76)
may be included or substituted.*

GATHERING

WORDS OF GRACE *One or more of the following:*

Blessed be the God who consoles us in all our affliction,
  so that we may be able to console those who are in any
    affliction
with the consolation
  with which we ourselves are consoled by God.
(2 CORINTHIANS 1:3a, 4)

Thus says the Lord:
A voice is heard in Ramah, lamentation and bitter weeping.
Rachel is weeping for her children;
she refuses to be comforted for her children,
because they are no more. (JEREMIAH 31:15)

The Lord is merciful and gracious,
  slow to anger and abounding in steadfast love.
As a father shows compassion to his children,
  so the Lord shows compassion to the faithful.
For the Lord knows our frame, and remembers that we are dust.
But the steadfast love of the Lord

is from everlasting to everlasting upon the faithful,
and the righteousness of the Lord to children's children,
    to those who keep his covenant
        and remember to do his commandments.
(PSALM 103:8, 13-14, 17-18, *UMH* 824-25)

PRAYER *One or more of the following:*

Life-giving God,
    your love surrounded each of us in our mothers' wombs,
    and from that secret place you called us forth to life.
Pour out your compassion upon *mother's Name.*
Her heart is heavy with the loss of the promise
    that once took form in her womb.
Have compassion upon *Names of father and/or other family
    members.*
Their hearts are also heavy with the loss of promise.
They grieve the death of the hopes *they (she)* anticipated,
    the dreams *they (she)* envisioned,
    the relationship *they (she)* desired.
Give *them (her)* the courage to admit *their (her)* pain and confusion,
    and couple that confession with the simplicity to rest in your
        care.
Allow *them (her)* to grieve, and then to accept this loss.
Warm *them (her)* with the embrace of your arms.
Knit together *their (her)* frayed emotions,
and bind *their (her)* heart(s)
    with the fabric of your love for *them (her).*
In the strong name of Jesus Christ we pray. **Amen.**

Lord, we do not understand why this life,
    which we had hoped to bring into this world,
    is now gone from us.
We only know that where there was sweet expectation,
    now there is bitter disappointment;
where there were hope and excitement,
    there is a sense of failure and loss.
We have seen how fragile life is,
and nothing can replace this life, this child, whom we have loved
    before seeing, before feeling it stirring in the womb,
    even before it was conceived.
In our pain and confusion we look to you, Lord,
    in whom no life is without meaning, however small or brief.
Let not our limited understanding confine our faith.
Draw us closer to you and closer to one another.

Lay our broken hearts open in faith to you
and in ever greater compassion to one another.
So raise us from death to life; we pray in Christ's name. **Amen.**

Ever-loving and caring God,
we come before you humbled by the mysteries of life and
death.
Help us to accept what we cannot understand,
to have faith where reason fails,
to have courage in the midst of disappointment.
Comfort *mother's Name,* who has lost a part of herself,
and *Names of father and/or other family members.*
Help *them (her)* to see the hope of life beyond grief.
Through Jesus we know that you love all your children
and are with us always.
Let us feel that presence now as we seek to live in faith,
through Jesus Christ our Lord. **Amen.**

SCRIPTURE *Suggested lessons:*

2 Samuel 12:15*b*-23	David and the death of his child
Isaiah 25:6-9	God will wipe away the tears.
Psalm 23 (*UMH* 754, 137)	The good shepherd
Psalm 42 (*UMH* 777)	Longing for God's presence
Psalm 90 (*UMH* 809)	God's eternal presence
Psalm 103 (*UMH* 824)	The steadfast love of God
Psalm 118 (*UMH* 839	God's love endures forever.
Psalm 121 (*UMH* 844)	From where will my help come?
Psalm 130 (*UMH* 515, 516, 848)	Out of the depths I cry.
Psalm 139 (*UMH* 854)	Where can I flee?
Romans 14:7-8	Living or dying, we are the Lord's.
1 Thessalonians 4:13-18	Do not grieve as those who have no hope.
1 John 3:1-2	See what love the Father has given us.
Matthew 5:1-12	The Beatitudes
Matthew 11:25-30	God revealed to babes
Matthew 18:1-5, 10-14	Children are greatest in God's kingdom.
Mark 10:13-16	Let the little children come to me.
John 14:1-6*a*	Do not let your hearts be troubled.

WITNESS

*Pastor, family, and friends may briefly voice their feelings and
Christian witness.*

Signs of faith, hope, and love may be exchanged.

PRAYER *One or both of the following may be used:*

Lord God, as your Son, Jesus,

took children into his arms and blessed them,
so we commit this child *Name* into your loving care.
Grant us the assurance that you have received this life,
which you gave,
and grant that when we stand before you
we might be as innocent and trusting as little children. **Amen.**

Compassionate God,
soothe the heart(s) of *Name(s)* and enlighten *their (her)* faith.

Give hope *to their hearts* and peace to *their lives.*
Grant mercy to *all members of this family (her)*
and comfort *them (her)* with the hope
that one day we shall all live with you,
through Jesus Christ our Lord. **Amen.**

*Here or elsewhere in the service a familiar and beloved hymn of
comfort may be sung.*

THE LORD'S PRAYER

BLESSING

MINISTRY WITH PERSONS
GOING THROUGH DIVORCE

Prayer

God of infinite love and understanding,
pour out your healing Spirit upon *Name,*
as *he/she* reflects upon the failure of *his/her* marriage
and makes a new beginning.
Where there is hurt or bitterness,
grant healing of memories
and the ability to put behind the things that are past.
Where feelings of despair or worthlessness flood in,
nurture the spirit of hope and confidence
that by your grace tomorrow can be better than yesterday.
Where *he/she* looks within and discovers faults
that have contributed to the destruction of the marriage
and have hurt other people,
grant forgiveness for what is past
and growth in all that makes for new life.
[Heal *children's names,* and help us minister your healing to *them.*]
We pray for [other] family and friends,
for the healing of their hurts and the acceptance of new

realities.
All this we ask in the name of the One
who sets us free from slavery to the past
and makes all things new,
even Jesus Christ our Savior. **Amen.**

Suggested Scripture Readings

Philippians 3:12-16	Press forward.
Luke 7:36-50	Jesus forgives a woman in the city.
Luke 13:10-17	Jesus heals a woman bent over.
Luke 18:35-43	Jesus heals a blind beggar.

MINISTRY WITH PERSONS SUFFERING FROM ADDICTION OR SUBSTANCE ABUSE

Prayer

God of mercy,
we bless you in the name of your Son, Jesus Christ,
who ministered to all who came to him.
Give your strength to *Name,* your servant,
[bound by the chains of addiction].
Enfold *him/her* in your love
and restore *him/her* to the freedom of your children.
Look with compassion on all those
who have lost their health and freedom.
Restore to them the assurance of your unfailing mercy.
Strengthen them in the work of recovery,
[and help them to resist all temptation].
To those who care for them,
grant patient understanding and a love that perseveres.
We ask this through Christ our Lord. **Amen.**

See also The Serenity Prayer (UMH 459).

Suggested Scripture Readings

2 Kings 5:1-14	Healing of Naaman by Elisha
Isaiah 63:7-9	God has mercifully favored us.
Psalm 121 (*UMH* 844)	My help comes from the Lord.
Psalm 130 (*UMH* 515, 516, 848)	Out of the depths
Romans 8:18-25	Present sufferings and future glory
Matthew 15:21-28	Woman, you have great faith.
Matthew 17:14-21	Jesus heals an epileptic boy.
Luke 4:31-37	Man with unclean spirit

MINISTRY WITH PERSONS WITH AIDS

Prayer

Most merciful God, you hold each of us dear to your heart.
Hold *Name(s)* in your loving arms
   and tenderly draw *them* into your love,
     together with all who are living with AIDS and HIV infection.
Assure them that they are not alone,
   and give them courage and faith for all that is to come.
Strengthen those who care for them and treat them,
   and guide those who do research.
Forgive those who have judged harshly,
   and enlighten those who live in prejudice or fear.
Nourish those who have lost sight of you,
   and heal the spirits of those who are broken.
We pray this in the name of Jesus, who suffered and died,
   and then rose from the dead to lead us into new life,
     now and for ever. **Amen.**

Suggested Scripture Readings

Psalm 13 (*UMH* 746)	Trust in the midst of suffering
Psalm 121 (*UMH* 844)	My help comes from the Lord.
Psalm 130 (*UMH* 515, 516, 848)	Out of the depths
Romans 8:31-39	Nothing can separate us from God's love.
Colossians 1:11-20	May you be strengthened with all power.
1 Peter 2:21-25	By Christ's wounds you have been healed.
Matthew 5:1-16	The Beatitudes
Matthew 8:1-4	The healing of a leper
Mark 2:1-12	Rise, take your mat, and go.
Luke 10:25-37	The good Samaritan
Luke 17:11-19	The healing of the ten lepers

MINISTRY WITH PERSONS WITH LIFE-THREATENING ILLNESS

Prayer

Lord Jesus Christ,
   we come to you sharing the suffering that you endured.
Grant us patience during this time,
   that as we and *Name* live with pain,
     disappointment, and frustration,
   we may realize that suffering is a part of life,
   a part of life that you know intimately.

Touch *Name* in *his/her* time of trial,
   hold *him/her* tenderly in your loving arms,
   and let *him/her* know you care.
Renew us in our spirits,
   even when our bodies are not being renewed,
   that we might be ever prepared to dwell in your eternal home,
through our faith in you, Lord Jesus,
   who died and are alive for evermore. **Amen.**

Suggested Scripture Readings

Ecclesiastes 3:1-11a	For everything there is a season.
Isaiah 25:6-10	God will swallow up death.
Psalm 23	The Lord is my shepherd.
Psalm 42	My soul longs for you.
Romans 8:18-25	Present sufferings and future glory
Romans 14:7-9	We are the Lord's.

*Familiar beloved hymns, or hymns suggested under Hymn of Healing
(100), may be sung to or with persons having a life-threatening illness.*

See also the resources in Ministry with the Dying (70-71).

MINISTRY WITH PERSONS
IN COMA OR UNABLE TO COMMUNICATE

Prayer

Eternal God, you have known us before we were here
   and will continue to know us after we are gone.
Touch *Name* with your grace and presence.
As you give your abiding care,
   assure *him/her* of our love and presence.
Assure *him/her* that our communion together remains secure,
   and that your love for *him/her* is unfailing.
In Christ, who came to us, we pray. **Amen.**

Suggested Scripture Readings

Psalm 23 (*UMH* 137)	The Lord is my shepherd.
Psalm 42 (*UMH* 777)	My soul longs for you.
Isaiah 61:1-3	The Spirit of the Lord
Romans 8:18-25	Present sufferings and future glory
Romans 14:7-9	We are the Lord's.

*Familiar beloved hymns may be sung to persons in coma or unable to
communicate.*

ACKNOWLEDGMENTS

GENERAL SERVICES

Abingdon Press; 2222 Rosa L. Parks Boulevard, Nashville, TN 37228-1306

68 Prayer #3 For an Untimely or Tragic Death, adapt. from *Lift Up Your Hearts* by Walter Russell Bowie, 1939; renewal © 1984 Jean B. Evans, Elizabeth Chapman, and Walter Russell Bowie, Jr. Used by permission of Abingdon Press.

Forward Movement Publications; 412 Sycamore St.; Cincinnati, OH 45202-4195.

42 Marriage Anniversary Prayer #2, adapt. from *Prayers for All Occasions*, © 1964 Forward Movement Publications. Used by permission.

International Commission on English in the Liturgy, Inc.; 1275 K St., NW, #1202; Washington, DC 20005-4097.

29-30 Wedding Post-communion Prayer, alt., text from *The Roman Missal* © 1973 ICEL. All rights reserved.

42 Marriage Anniversary Prayer #1, alt., text from *The Roman Missal* © 1973, ICEL. All rights reserved.

Methodist Publishing House; 20, Ivattway; Peterborough PE3 7PG; England.

38 Declaration by the Husband and Wife, adapt. from *The Methodist Service Book* © The Methodist Conference 1975. Used by permission of Methodist Publishing House.

Morehouse Publishing; 871 Ethan Allen Highway; Ridgefield, CT 06877.

67 Prayer #1 For an Untimely or Tragic Death and

70 prayer #5 At the Service for a Person Who Did Not Profess the Christian Faith from *Burial Services* © 1980 Joseph Buchanan Bernardin. Used by permission of Morehouse Publishing.

The Uniting Church in Australia Assembly Commission on Liturgy; c/o Ian Culliman; 29 Menin Rd.; Corinda, Queensland, 4075; Australia.

72 Prayer #4 in Ministry Immediately Following Death, alt., from UNITING IN WORSHIP LEADER'S BOOK, © 1988, UCAACL. Used by permission of The Joint Board of Christian Education, Melbourne, Australia.

Westminster/John Knox Press; 100 Witherspoon St.; Louisville, KY 40202-1396.

39 Declaration of Marriage, adapt., reprinted from THE WORSHIP BOOK: Services and Hymns. © MCMLXX, MCMLXXII, The Westminster Press. Used by permission of Westminster/John Knox Press.

37 Greeting, adapt., reprinted from THE WORSHIP BOOK: Services and Hymns. © MCMLXX, MCMLXXII, The Westminster Press. Used by permission of Westminster/John Knox Press.

71-72 Prayer #1 in Ministry Immediately Following Death, alt., reprinted from THE FUNERAL: A Service of Witness to the Resurrection (Supplemental

Liturgical Resource 4). © 1986 The Westminster Press. Used by permission of Westminster/John Knox Press.

71 Prayer #2 in Ministry with the Dying, reprinted from THE FUNERAL: A Service of Witness to the Resurrection (Supplemental Liturgical Resource 4). © 1986 The Westminster Press. Used by permission of Westminster/John Knox Press.

Wm. B. Eerdmans Publishing Co.; 255 Jefferson Ave. SE; Grand Rapids, MI 49503.

67 Prayer #2 for An Untimely or Tragic Death adapt. from "When Death Intrudes Untimely . . . an individual prayer" in *Dialogues with God* by O. Thomas Miles, Wm. B. Eerdmans Publishing Co.

DAILY PRAISE AND PRAYER

Central Conference of American Rabbis; 192 Lexington Ave.; New York, NY 10016.

85-86 Prayer of Thanksgiving #2, "Jewish Prayer for Divine Providence" in *Gates of Prayer*, p. 35, 1975, CCAR.

Christian Conference of Asia Youth; G/F.; 2 Jordan Road; Kowloon; Hong Kong.

82-83 Prayer of Thanksgiving #2, from "Your Will Be Done," 1985, CCA Youth.

77-78 Prayer of Thanksgiving #2, alt. from "Your Will Be Done," 1985, CCA Youth.

International Commission on English in the Liturgy, Inc.; 1275 K St., NW, #1202; Washington, DC 20005-4097.

80 Prayer of Thanksgiving text from *The Liturgy of the Hours* © 1974, ICEL. All rights reserved.

85 Prayer of Thanksgiving #1 text from *The Liturgy of the Hours* © 1974, ICEL. All rights reserved.

Order of Saint Luke Publications; 5246 Broadway; Cleveland, OH 44127-1500.

86 Commendation, alt., from The Book of Offices and Services After the Usage of The Order of Saint Luke, Timothy J. Crouch, O.S.L. ed. and comp. Cleveland (OSL Publications) © 1988. Used by permission.

Westminster/John Knox Press; 100 Witherspoon Street; Louisville, KY 40202.

77 Prayer of Thanksgiving #1 reprinted from THE WORSHIPBOOK: Services and Hymns, © MCMLXX, MCMLXXII, The Westminster Press. Used by permission of Westminster/John Knox Press.

William G. Storey; 1027 East Wayne Ave.; South Bend, IN 46617.

82 Prayer of Thanksgiving #1 trans. Wm. G. Storey from the Greek.

OCCASIONAL SERVICES

Consultation on Church Union; 151 Wall Street; Princeton, NJ 08540-1514.

88-89 Prayer of Thanksgiving for the Adoption of a Child; Prayer of Thanksgiving for the Birth of a Child; and Prayer of Thanksgiving for the Family from An Order of Thanksgiving for the Birth or Adoption of a Child, by the Commission on Worship of the Consultation on Church Union. © 1980 by Consultation on Church Union.

Timothy J. Crouch, O.S.L.; 5246 Broadway; Cleveland, OH 44127-1500

90 Opening Prayer © 1989 Timothy J. Crouch, O.S.L.

HEALING SERVICES AND PRAYERS

The Christian Century Foundation; 407 S. Dearborn St.; Chicago, IL 60605-1111.

103-6 A Service of Hope after Loss of Pregnancy, portions adapt. from "Service of Hope" by Karen Westerfield Tucker. © 1989 CHRISTIAN CENTURY FOUNDATION. Reprinted by permission from the January-February 1989 issue of *The Christian Ministry*.

The English Language Liturgical Consultation; 1275 K St., NW, #1202; Washington, DC 20005.

97 Sursum Corda, alt., from the English trans. of "Lift up your hearts" prepared by ELLC 1988.

International Commission on English in the Liturgy; 1275 K St., NW, Suite 1202; Washington, DC 20005.

106 Closing Prayer #2, alt., text from *The Book of Blessings* © 1988, ICEL. All rights reserved.

98 Memorial Acclamation text from *The Roman Missal* © 1973, ICEL. All rights reserved.

The International Consultation on English Texts; 1275 K St., NW. #1202; Washington, DC 20005-4097.

97 Sanctus and Benedictus from the English trans. of the Sanctus/Benedictus by ICET.

Order of Saint Luke Publications; 5246 Broadway; Cleveland, OH 44127-1500.

101 Dismissal with Blessing, alt., from The Book of Offices and Services After the Usage of The Order of Saint Luke, Timothy J. Crouch, O.S.L. ed. and comp. Cleveland (OSL Publications) © 1988. Used by permission.

United Church of Christ Office for Church Life and Leadership; 700 Prospect Avenue East; Cleveland, OH 44115.

102 Confession and Pardon from *Book of Worship* © 1986.

United States Catholic Conference; 3211 Fourth Street, N.E.; Washington, DC 20017-1194.

107 Addiction Prayer, alt., additional blessings from the **Book of Blessings** for use in the United States of America © 1988, by USCC, Washington, D.C. are used with permission. All rights reserved.

Westminster/John Knox Press; 100 Witherspoon Street; Louisville, KY 40202-1396.

109 Prayer with Persons in Coma, alt., reprinted from SERVICES FOR OCCASIONS OF PASTORAL CARE (Supplemental Liturgical Resource, p. 69.). © 1990 Westminster/John Knox Press. Used by permission.